Ageing, Spirituality and Well-being

of related interest

Spirituality and Ageing
Edited by Albert Jewell
ISBN 1 85302 631 X

The Spiritual Dimension of Ageing
Elizabeth MacKinlay
ISBN 1 84310 008 8

Hearing the Voice of People with Dementia
Opportunities and Obstacles
Malcolm Goldsmith
ISBN 1 85302 406 6

Spiritual Caregiving as Secular Sacrament
A Practical Theology for Professional Caregivers
Ray S. Anderson
ISBN 1 84310 746 5

In Living Color
An Intercultural Approach to Pastoral Care and Counseling
Second Edition
Emmanuel Y. Lartey
ISBN 1 84310 750 3

A Guide to the Spiritual Dimension of Care for People
with Alzheimer's Disease and Related Dementia
More than Body, Brain and Breath
Eileen Shamy
ISBN 1 84310 129 7

Spirituality in Health Care Contexts
Edited by Helen Orchard
ISBN 1 85302 969 6

Spirituality, Healing and Medicine
Return to the Silence
David Aldridge
ISBN 1 85302 554 2

Spiritual Dimensions of Pastoral Care
Practical Theology in a Multidisciplinary Context
Edited by David Willows and John Swinton
ISBN 1 85302 892 4

Ageing, Spirituality and Well-being

Edited by Albert Jewell

Jessica Kingsley Publishers
London and New York

First published in the United Kingdom in 2004
by Jessica Kingsley Publishers Ltd
116 Pentonville Road
London N1 9JB, England
and
29 West 35th Street, 10th fl.
New York, NY 10001-2299, USA

www.jkp.com

Copyright © Jessica Kingsley Publishers 2004

Library of Congress Cataloging in Publication Data
A CIP catalog record for this book is available from the Library of Congress

British Library Cataloguing in Publication Data
A CIP catalogue record for this book is available from the British Library

ISBN 1 84310 167 X

Printed and Bound in Great Britain by
Athenaeum Press, Gateshead, Tyne and Wear

Contents

Preface

Albert Jewell

Having edited *Spirituality and Ageing* (1999), I count it a privilege to act in the same capacity for this publication. The provenance however is different. The first book arose out of the Sir Halley Stewart project of which I was the administrator. The purpose of that project was to raise awareness of the spiritual needs of older people and encourage interest in the spirituality of ageing in the church and the wider community in the UK. Some four years later a great deal has been achieved towards that end. Further publications have burgeoned. Ageing is seen as a very important social issue and spirituality is on the agenda of many more people than those who attend church, synagogue, mosque or temple.

The present book arose out of the Second International Conference on Ageing, Spirituality and Well-being held at Durham University in July 2002. The first such conference was held in Canberra in 2000 and the UK delegates representing the Christian Council on Ageing (CCOA) were asked to make arrangements for the 2002 conference. MHA Care Group (formerly known as Methodist Homes for the Aged), which I served first as Pastoral Director and then as Senior Chaplain, were invited to co-sponsor the event along with CCOA and provide the necessary administrative back-up. This they did largely thanks to the dedicated work of Mrs Lynn Fox, who acted as my PA until my retirement in 2001 and who now serves in the same capacity for my successor, Rev Dr Keith Albans, who himself worked tirelessly behind the scenes at Durham.

Some 200 people attended the conference and were treated to keynote addresses, papers and workshops of a very high quality. This book brings together all of the plenary addresses, rewritten for publication, plus a selection of the other papers, though sadly the workshops do not lend themselves easily to such reproduction.

In Chapter 5 Elizabeth MacKinlay has compressed the material which can be read in full in her book *The Spiritual Dimension of Ageing* (2001a) and has updated it.

Earlier versions of Chapter 8 by Leo Missinne previously appeared in *Quarterly Papers on Religion*, vol. 1, no. 5, published by St Paul School of Theology, Kansas City, Missouri, and in *Spiritual Well-being of the Elderly* (eds J. A. Thorson and T. C. Cook) (1980), published by C. C. Thomas of Springfield, Illinois. We are grateful to the college and to the publishers for permission to reproduce here.

Dr Krishna Mohan wishes to place on record his sincere thanks to Dr Daphne Wallace, chair of the CCOA Dementia Group, for her help in preparing his chapter for publication.

In some ways the book that has now been produced provides even richer fare than the original event. Two main speakers were hospitalised and had to drop out of the conference late in the day. Rev Malcolm Goldsmith, who had so excited the Canberra conference, has kindly written up what he would have said in his address under the evocative title 'The Stars Only Shine in the Night'. Professor John Hull of Birmingham University would have spoken about his experience of blindness. In place of this, and because the physical aspects of ageing ought not to be ignored, I asked Penelope Wilcock, a contributor to *Spirituality and Ageing*, if she would write Chapter 4 about the challenge of stroke. This she has done to great effect.

I have also written an introductory chapter that provides fuller information about MHA Care Group and CCOA, looks at some of the definitions of spirituality offered by the other writers and suggests a possible model.

We invited the Rt Revd Dr David Jenkins, former Professor of Theology in the University of Leeds and Bishop of Durham from 1984–1994, to keep a watching brief at the conference and in the final keynote address to share with us his reflections. He has now rewritten these as 'reflections on reflections', in a most stimulating and provocative 'endpiece' (Chapter 14). Readers of the earlier chapters will have to decide how fair he has been in his critique, but he certainly makes a trenchant case.

What no book can do, of course, is to replicate the debates that the addresses and papers generate at a conference and the general 'buzz' of so many people from many different disciplines and the churches getting together. I trust nonetheless that what is written will be seen as a worthy contribution to the ongoing discussion about the part played by spirituality in the well-being of older people.

CHAPTER 1

Nourishing the Inner Being

A Spirituality Model

Albert Jewell

As General Editor my aims in this first chapter are threefold. First I shall give some background information about the two organisations which sponsored the Second International Conference on Ageing, Spirituality and Well-being held at Durham University in July 2002. Next I shall comment upon the different interpretations of the word 'spirituality' offered by the contributors to this book and consider what are the spiritual needs of older people. Finally I want to introduce the spirituality model (together with the thinking that lies behind it) developed by MHA (Methodist Homes for the Aged) Care Group, whose recently produced training video, *Nourishing the Inner Being*, provides the title for this first chapter.

MHA Care Group

Founded as Methodist Homes for the Aged (MHA) 60 years ago, the organisation was early in the field of providing high quality residential care in the UK. From the outset incoming residents were encouraged to bring as much of their own furniture and effects as could reasonably be accommodated, were always allotted single rooms, benefited from the services of a chaplain and volunteers mainly drawn from local churches, and had the opportunity to participate if they wished in worship and fellowship on a regular or occasional basis. The service provided was never intended just for Methodists, and since the implementation of the care in the community legislation in the UK there has been an increasing diversification in those seeking MHA care. Today there are over 40 residential and nursing homes in England and Wales.

The services offered have also been diversified over the past 25 years: into specialised dementia care, sheltered housing provision (including Scotland) and home-based support from volunteers through 'Live at Home Schemes' in various parts of England and Wales. It was this diversification that led to major changes in governance and the creation of MHA Care Group in 2001.

MHA Care Group is committed to providing care and services for older people to the highest professional standards undergirded by Christian values. In November 2002 its mission and its values were redefined as follows.

Our mission

To improve the quality of life for older people, inspired by Christian concern.

What we stand for

The following values underpin the way in which we seek to fulfil this mission:

- We will strive for *excellence* in everything we do.
- We will meet everyone's *spiritual needs* along with their other needs.
- We will *respect* every person as a unique individual.
- We will treat others with the *dignity* we wish for ourselves.
- We will encourage *personal growth and development*.
- We will *care for one another*, especially the most frail and vulnerable.
- We will be *open and fair* in all our dealings.

Putting our values into practice

We are open to all older people in need, irrespective of their beliefs. Our homes and schemes are made up of diverse communities. Opportunities are made available for individuals to develop and practise their faith as they feel appropriate.

A special feature of our homes and schemes is the emphasis placed on the spiritual well-being of older people. We believe this to be an important element of the service we provide and an integral part of everybody's work.

We respect the personal beliefs of each individual, and the choice of older people to participate, or not, in activities and events within the home or scheme.

It is important that all our staff, volunteers and those we serve understand and share our values in order to play their part in building a community which delivers an improved quality of life for older people.

Christian Council on Ageing

Co-sponsor of the Second International Conference was the Christian Council on Ageing (CCOA). A registered charity formed 20 years ago, it has as its patrons leaders of most of the main Christian denominations in the UK and declares the following aims:

1. To explore the Christian potential and vocation in later years, and to nurture the continuing development of personal faith and growth.

2. To affirm the contribution of older people to their local church and community and to encourage wider understanding across the generations.

3. To improve the pastoral care of, and the opportunities for worship and fellowship for, frail and elderly people.

4. To improve pastoral support and fellowship for those who care for elderly people.

5. To co-operate with other agencies concerned with ageing, including those of other faiths.

6. To encourage an educated response to ageism in the churches.

The intention of CCOA is to be as inclusive and ecumenical as possible. In pursuance of its aims CCOA has published an impressive list of booklets (occasional papers and good practice guides), produced a number of audio-tapes, and held regular conferences in various parts of the country. CCOA has taken a special interest in the holistic care of people with dementia, setting up two successive Newcastle-based dementia projects and producing an acclaimed video on the subject, *Is Anyone There?* CCOA has worked with MHA Care Group, Faith in Elderly People (Leeds) and others, notably in the publications of the Halley Stewart Age Awareness Project and more recently: *Spiritual Care: Guidelines for Care Plans* (Hammond and Moffitt 2000); *Frequently Asked Questions on Spirituality and Religion* (Airey *et al.* 2002); *Religious Practice and People with Dementia* (Moffitt and Allen 2002) with its interfaith perspective.

What is spirituality?

'Spirituality' is of course a notoriously slippery term. In Chapter 14, David Jenkins goes so far as to call it 'a weasel word'. It can be interpreted so broadly as to lose any distinctiveness or so narrowly as to appear to exclude large numbers of people. It was remarked by a number of those attending the Durham international conference that the word was defined so differently by the various keynote speakers that it might have been better had there been an agreed definition from the outset so that there was common ground.

As one of the organisers of the conference I beg to disagree. The different definitions offered fairly represent a cross-section of the various understandings of the word that have emerged in recent years. The authors of the chapters in this book would rightly have demurred had they been asked to adopt a common 'party line'. I would argue that such a breadth of understanding serves to reinforce the inclusive nature of this dimension of being human and gives everyone room to 'breathe'.

However, the writers share much common ground. Most of the main contributors to this book distinguish between 'spirituality', which is seen as universal, and the narrower concept of 'religion', whilst accepting that for many people their spirituality will be expressed within the framework of a particular religion, or at least include the notion of a divine being. Rosalie Hudson's working of this out in relation to the Christian doctrine of the Trinity (Chapter 6) is a fine example of the latter approach. Krishna Mohan does the same in relation to Indian religions in Chapter 12.

For Elizabeth MacKinlay (Chapter 5) spirituality is 'that which lies at the core of each person's being, an essential dimension which brings meaning to life'. She contends that it must be understood more broadly than religious practices: '...as relationship with God, however God or ultimate meaning is perceived...and in relationship with other people'. Spirituality is far from being a private and self-centred matter. Harriet Mowat (Chapter 3) similarly argues this point. This is brought home powerfully by Penelope Wilcock (Chapter 4) in relation to those who have suffered strokes and who are so dependent upon the understanding and encouragement of other people if their personhood is to be maintained or restored. John Killick (Chapter 10) argues the same regarding people with dementia. Whilst, perhaps wisely, avoiding the actual word 'spirituality', Leo Missinne (Chapter 8), like Elizabeth MacKinlay, identifies the search for meaning in life as the sine qua non of being human.

Depth and ultimacy also find their place in the definition favoured by Deborah Dunn (Chapter 11), whose quotation from Kathleen Fischer fills out the adversity and challenge through which a person's spirituality must 'cut its teeth', as it were:

> Spirituality means not just one compartment of life, but the deepest dimension of all life. The spiritual is the ultimate ground of all our questions, hope, fears, and loves... It concerns our struggles with loss; questions of self-worth and fear of reaching out to make new friendships. (Fischer 1998, p.13)

Perhaps it is Ursula King's preferred definition (Chapter 9) that is most pertinent for older people who may be facing diminishment on various fronts. She sees spirituality as '*spiritual development, a process of growth* that can still flourish when all other growth has stopped and our physical and mental powers begin to decline'. Harriet Mowat (Chapter 3) is in agreement as she spells out the complex relationship between spirituality and 'successful ageing' that should be regarded as a spiritual journey towards wholeness which can transcend what is usually regarded as ill health and adversity.

John Killick (Chapter 10), who like Missinne eschews the actual word 'spirituality', movingly shows how crucially important continued artistic and poetic creativity can be for people with dementia – and that it is wrong to suppose that such creative expression is now beyond their capability. This is a message of hope indeed.

David Jenkins, adopting a rather different approach in the final chapter, challenges the excessively esoteric and goes so far as to suggest 'getting help and getting by' as a down-to-earth definition of spirituality, encouraging a spirit of self-help on the part of ageing people who have so much to offer and urging a greatly increased sense of what living in community is all about.

Holistic personhood

In the remainder of this chapter I want to present how one organisation (MHA Care Group) has come to understand the spiritual dimension and seeks to make appropriate provision of spiritual care. Those appointed as care home managers are asked to be in sympathy with the Christian values of the organisation stated above and to ensure that the spiritual needs of residents are recognised and met within a holistic model of care.

The thinking upon which this is based is represented diagrammatically in Figure 1.1. The various needs of individual persons (physical, mental, emotional, social, spiritual, etc.) can be perceived in separation one from the other – as different 'bits' of each individual – as depicted in (a). Such separation is valuable only in that it helps to identify these different needs, one or other of which can easily be overlooked or neglected. Such rigid variegation however makes a travesty of individual personhood. Somewhat of an improvement is (b), which represents these same needs as different aspects (or dimensions) of a person. However, such a vertical 'carving up' of the person is not a lot better than the horizontal one. Neither is truly 'holistic' (see Chapter 6).

Commenting on the work of the National Interfaith Conference on Ageing in the USA, Thorson and Cook (1980, p.xiii) declare: 'The spiritual is not one dimension among many in life; rather, it permeates and gives meaning to all life.' In an unpublished paper, 'Challenging Depression – Taking a Spiritually Enhanced Approach', retired Australian geriatrician Murray Lloyd (2003) develops this idea and presents a circular holistic model of the human being comprising four segments (emotional, social, physical, cognitive), the heart of the circle feeding each segment being the

HOLISTIC PERSONHOOD

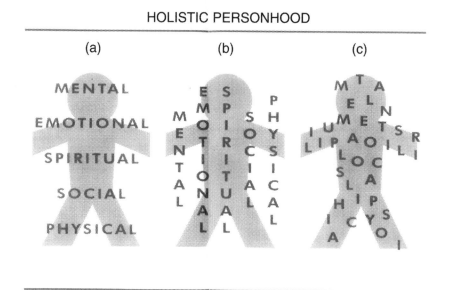

Figure 1.1 The spiritual needs of older people

human spirit as 'the centre of energy whose core function is to give continuing meaning to our lives and nourishment to our inner being'.

A holistic view is therefore not so much concerned with identifying the sum total or hierarchy of human needs as with acknowledging that in each person all these needs are inextricably intermixed as in Figure 1.1 (c). None can be addressed in separation or isolation from the others. This is true to ancient Hebrew thought in which body, mind, spirit are seen as interpenetrative of each other and not as separate parts of the one multifaceted person. It was Greek thought that created the separation of body, mind and soul that has tended to dominate medical practice and social care (as well as theology) through much of the history of the western world and is still widely entrenched today.

Spiritual needs

What then are spiritual needs if they do not relate to some separate and identifiable part of the human person? In a nutshell, and building upon the definitions of spirituality noted above, they are those needs that relate to the inner being of every person and give to that person continuing meaning and purpose in life and the strength to go on living. The intangibles in life that make living more than merely existing or, as Pamela Lynn Schultz-Hipp puts it, 'the human awareness of a relationship or connection that goes beyond sensory perceptions' (2001, p.86). Such intangibles will impact upon health of body. They will have mental and emotional aspects and – in that humans are social beings – cannot be fulfilled in isolation. In this sense every person is a spiritual being, whether they recognise it or not in such terms, and whether or not they believe in a divine being or power.

In the thinking of MHA Care Group, whatever the age of the person, the following are some of the most significant:

1. The need to receive and give *love* (intentionally seen that way round in that it is because we receive love that we know how to, and desire to, give love). Christians go so far as to say 'We love because God first loves us' (I John 4:19), but this love is most obviously mediated through other people. As Joanne Armatowski puts it: 'It is difficult to experience [this divine acceptance] unless God's love is mediated through genuine human love from others' (2001, p.78).

2. The need to sustain *hope*: something to look forward to day by day and in relation to longer term purposes, plans and dreams. The eighteenth-century English poet Alexander Pope declared that 'Hope springs eternal in the human breast'. Humans do indeed seem to have the capacity to hope against hope, even in the most adverse circumstances. Those with a personal religious faith very often have a perspective that goes beyond the confines of this earthly life and places ultimate hope for something beyond in God. Malcolm Goldsmith (Chapter 2) writes powerfully of the stars of hope that people discover when the light fades and night-time comes.

3. The need for something or someone to believe in – *faith/trust*. This may not be a divine being or power but people do seem to have a need to live for something or someone beyond themselves. Aside from money and other material considerations, faith may be placed in other people (whether close to or distant from the one placing his/her trust), one's country or group, political parties or systems, religious creeds,

and of course most people will have values or principles by which they seek to live their lives.

4. The need for *creativity*: to develop skills and talents to make something of the raw material of the world and of one's life. This may be severely practical or sublimely aesthetic. Primitive man-made tools, weapons and shelters but also fashioned wall paintings and jewellery. The Judaeo-Christian tradition sees this as a reflection of the divine creator in whose image men and women are believed to have been made. Whether or not a person believes this, creativity brings great joy and satisfaction to so many human beings.

5. The need for at least a reasonable degree of *peace*. This peace is one not just of circumstance (which can never be guaranteed) but of heart and mind. The seventeenth-century poet George Herbert in his poem 'The Pulley' recognised that human beings seek and strive for rest – but, if it were given from the outset, that would cut the nerve of human endeavour. St Augustine of Hippo (CE 354–430) is credited with the prayer: 'Lord, you have made us for yourself and our hearts are restless till they rest in you.' Whether believers or not, people often say of someone who has died that they are now 'at peace'.

To the extent to which these basic human needs are met, people find continuing meaning, purpose and fulfilment for their lives. As Viktor Frankl (1984) reiterates, they can transcend the suffering that is an inevitable part of human existence. It is such adversity that demonstrates the 'spiritual take-home value' of the human needs we have identified.

But what about the spiritual needs of older people in particular? It would be spurious to maintain that these are any different from those of people of any age group. Human spiritual needs do not change as one lives through and completes the transitions relating to the so-called 'four ages' of human life. However, it would also be misguided not to recognise that these basic needs tend to be focused in very specific ways for those of more advanced years, and this for reasons both circumstantial and existential. The circumstances faced by the majority (if not all) of older people include losses and diminishments on a scale unknown in earlier life. Older people are also, whether explicitly or not, aware that death is that much nearer:

time-wise there is less of life ahead than heretofore. This inevitably changes the focus even if the basic facts of human life and death are unaltered. So perhaps these needs can be helpfully restated as follows for older people in the form of six '-ations':

1. *Isolation.* This of course is in reality the circumstance that gives rise to the need for human communication and companionship. As people enter advanced old age, family dispersal, the deaths of contemporary friends, changes of neighbours, hearing and sight loss and increasing immobility mean that many become cut off from normal regular contact with other people. Sometimes isolated older people can deter would-be callers because they seek to maximise opportunities and seem capable of speaking non-stop and at very great length. Many lament that there is no longer any physical contact with anyone: they can go for days without talking to anyone and for months without anyone actually touching them.

2. *Affirmation.* Many older people, having retired from their career and completed long ago the bringing up of their immediate family, can feel that life no longer has point or purpose. It is hard for them to believe that they are important to anyone any more, that they are in any way useful and that their contribution to society would be missed. Moreover no one seems interested in hearing their story, the telling of which would bring them some retrospective affirmation. It is no wonder that anomie or clinical depression are so common in this age group.

3. *Celebration.* It is a natural human instinct to want to share one's joy. Older people in many regards have so much more to celebrate than during other periods of life – special birthdays and anniversaries, lifetime achievements, the fruits of their creativity, rich memories and sheer survival for so long through thick and thin – yet few others willing or able to share their celebration, although of course a fuss may well be made when they are 90 or 100 or if their marriage survives 50 or 60 years.

4. *Confirmation.* It is a myth that most older people will face increasing frailty and the prospect of their demise with equanimity and, if they are religious believers, a serene hope of a life to come. Some of course will. However, the experience of ageing and the prospect of death are more likely to prompt troubling – indeed ultimate – questions and deep doubts: What, in the end, have I achieved? At the end of the day is it true, as the Old Testament writer of Ecclesiastes (1:2) puts it, that all is 'vanity', in the sense of emptiness? Have I worked, loved, believed in vain? Is death the end and, if not, will I be found worthy to enter the life to come and will I meet my loved ones there? They may not actually articulate such questions, which they fear are 'unworthy' or will rock the boat for other people, but they desperately need some confirmation of what they have in the past held so dear. It is this spiritual questioning in later life which Peter G. Coleman elaborates in Chapter 7 following a longitudinal study over 25 years.

5. *Reconciliation.* The often unexpressed hope of aged people is that they will die 'at peace', by which they mean reconciled to their loved ones, themselves and (if they are believers) their God. Everyone accumulates and carries emotional baggage through life, often associated with fallings out, feuds and deep regrets and remorse concerning close relationships. Older people need to shed this baggage before they die rather than it prevent a 'good death' and carry over to the funeral and beyond. Much of it has to do with other people who themselves may have died – maybe long ago – and they yearn for the healing of memories. Sometimes specialist help may be required through a counsellor, therapist or priest, but in many cases a good listener can be of enormous help, as several of the contributors to this book urge.

6. *Integration.* This is a word and concept that speaks of wholeness, of a coming together of a complete life, past, present and whatever future may remain. If it is true, as Elizabeth MacKinlay passionately believes and states in Chapter 5, that human beings are inveterate 'meaning makers', then they need

to make sense somehow of the whole of life, not just of the various periods of their life. They are very much in the business of 'final' and 'ultimate' meanings. It is not far removed from Erik Erikson's concept of the eighth stage of life being the resolution of the crisis of integrity versus despair and, from his wife Joan's addition of a conjectured ninth stage, that of gero-transcendence which is marked by the ultimate wisdom and integrity of human fulfilment (Erikson and Erikson 1997). It is worth noting that Elizabeth Kubler-Ross (1975) goes so far as to view the dying stage of life as being potentially the most profound growth event of all through which total integration may be achieved.

It is the belief of a Christian-based organisation such as MHA Care Group that all these spiritual needs focused in old age should be recognised and met as fully as possible. These identified needs can be fulfilled, in part, through caring human relationships without 'strings of faith' being attached. However, germane to the Christian gospel is the understanding that love, hope, peace and joy are the gifts of God. It is also recognised that the Christian community has a vital role in mediating these gifts through its fellowship, support and prayer – though they will always retain an eternal quality which points beyond humanity and beyond this life.

A spirituality model

To facilitate staff understanding and practice, MHA Care Group has evolved a spirituality model which is the outcome of several years of consideration and discussion both within the organisation and with other interested parties. It is this model that forms the focus of their training video *Nourishing the Inner Being*.

The model (Figure 1.2) is posited on a broad definition of spirituality as 'what gives continuing meaning and purpose to a person's life and nourishes their inner being'. Discovering what this may be in the case of every resident requires sensitive discussion and observation and is bound to reveal a great variety of indicators.

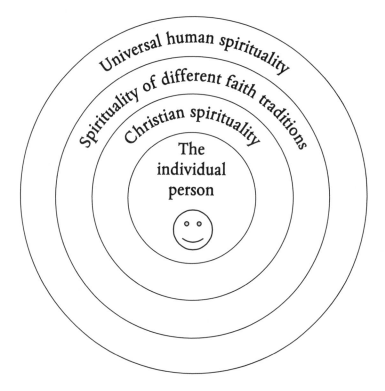

Well-being

- Love
- Hope
- Joy
- Creativity
- Peace

Ill-being

- Isolation
- Despair
- Sadness
- Boredom
- Anxiety

Figure 1.2 A spirituality model for MHA Care Group: Nourishing the inner being

The concentric circles need to be expounded from the outside in. The widest and most inclusive circle is that designated 'universal human spirituality'. As already argued, everyone, whether consciously or otherwise, is a spiritual being in the sense that there are multifarious 'invisible' or intangible qualities which are highly important to each and every person. These include personal values, relationships, the natural world, music, art, etc. The authors of *Spiritual Care: Guidelines for Care Plans* refer to 'moments of awe and wonder' which people experience through one or more of their senses (Hammond and Moffitt 2000). Some of these qualities will be found listed to the left below the concentric circle diagram and will be referred to again later.

Proceeding inwards, the next circle is again wide but not so expansive as the first. Very many, though certainly not all, human beings adhere to some form of religion and will find many of their spiritual needs fulfilled through the beliefs, rituals and practices of their particular faith tradition. Each major religion has its own 'spirituality' and sometimes several within the one faith family: one has only to think of Sunni, Shi-ite and Sufi Muslims, Theravada and Mahayana Buddhists, or Orthodox, Liberal, Reform and Hasidic Jews. The positive recognition of other faith traditions is a key plank in enabling MHA Care Group to work in partnership with organisations representative of those traditions in extending care provision to other ethnic groups.

A narrower circle represents the Christian religion within the whole conspectus of world faiths. It is the particular religious tradition within which most older people in the UK today will have some roots – though for how long this will continue is perhaps debatable. Christian spirituality of course also offers a whole variety of alternative forms each with their subgroups: Roman Catholic, Orthodox, Protestant, Pentecostal; evangelical, sacramental, charismatic and more contemplative forms of devotion. Though finding its place amongst mainstream Protestants, Methodism has its own emphases: its openness to 'all'; its view of the Christian life as an ever-developing one towards ultimate maturity; its joyful worship; its emphasis upon small fellowship or 'cell' groups, etc.

To date the great majority of MHA Care Group residents have belonged to the main Protestant Christian communities, with Methodists providing the largest subgroup. However, there are sometimes members of other faith traditions and of course many more whose adherence is of a more 'nominal' nature or who are agnostic – whilst of course still remaining spiritual beings.

The spiritual care provided by the organisation requires a sensitive awareness and application of the spiritual model, and in the document that accompanies the training video guidelines are set out for appropriate assessment and practice over a great variety of different scenarios. Care staff are encouraged to recognise that they are themselves spiritual beings and share with residents a common universal spirituality, and to discover what aspects are most significant in the case of each resident whose key worker they may be or become. (A similar approach is shared by Deborah Dunn in Chapter 11.) Detailed case studies are offered in the accompanying document. It is of course all-important that a sensitive assessment of the spiritual needs of each resident should be made – and that this should be reviewed at regular intervals, for neither 'spirituality' nor 'spiritual well-being' remain static.

Within a holistic care model it is important to see that the meeting of physical needs such as bathing and sharing meals has a spiritual aspect in that it is capable also of ministering to the deeper needs of residents if the practice is truly loving and affirming. This is well spelt out in the *Spiritual Care: Guidelines for Care Plans* document (Hammond and Moffitt 2000). Specialist pastoral and spiritual care are of course available to every resident through the chaplain, visiting ministers and representatives of their faith tradition, church-related volunteers, as well as the gifts and expertise of many of the residents themselves.

It must never be forgotten that at the heart of the concentric circle model (in the innermost circle) lies the individual person: the 'each' that counterbalances the 'all' of the widest circle. People will find their 'spiritual home' within one or other of the areas denoted by the concentric circles – perhaps within several. It is for their individual holistic well-being that the care home exists. It is imperative that their spiritual needs (along with their physical, mental, emotional and social needs) be met as far as possible as they themselves wish, both at the broadest and most specific levels. Of course the needs of each individual have to be held in balance with those of all the others who make up the resident community, the general ethos of which needs to be preserved and nourished.

Below the concentric model, to the left and right, are listed some of the qualities that make for individual well-being or ill-being. In fact they reflect what may be regarded as those most basic human spiritual needs indicated earlier in this chapter. Whilst it should not be maintained that in no circumstances can the 'negative' qualities to the right be conducive to personal growth (see Chapter 3) appropriate spiritual care will reduce them and encourage residents to experience their opposites – in other words to experience increasing well-being despite the diminutions of advancing years. It is in this hope that MHA Care Group offers its spirituality model to the wider community to consider and develop.

Further information regarding the spirituality model and the training video *Nourishing the Inner Being* may be obtained from:

Rev Dr Keith Albans
MHA Care Group
Epworth House
Stuart Street
Derby DE1 2EQ.

CCOA may be contacted c/o the same address.

CHAPTER 2

The Stars Only Shine in the Night
The Challenge of Creative Ageing

Malcolm Goldsmith

> We live in a society where ageing is often viewed as an embarrassment, suffering and dying a meaningless experience and death a medical failure. Older adults find themselves stranded in the unchartered territory of longer life expectancy with a pervasive bio-medical model of ageing, void of sacramental meaning. (Kimble 2002, p.40)

The first person I gave Holy Communion to after I was ordained over 40 years ago was Mary Robinson. I was a fresh young curate hitting the parish after five years at university; she was a frail old lady of 88. Looking back I think that meeting her was my first meaningful encounter with an elderly person apart from my grandmother, who wasn't quite as old. A few weeks after that communion service Mary Robinson fell in the street and lay in the gutter for quite some time before help arrived. She had broken her arm. Shortly afterwards I visited her and said something to the effect that it must have been awful for her and how was she coping. I shall always remember her reply: 'I regard it as a great privilege that at my age I am still able to share in the pain of the world.' This was not pious humbuggery but the considered comment of a remarkable lady.

I was later to discover that she did *The Times* crossword every day, never taking more than 18 minutes to complete it. Her younger sister, however, with whom she lived – a sprightly 86 years old – could complete it quicker than that and never needed to write down the solutions in the grid.

Mary and Margaret Robinson had deliberately chosen to come and live in one of the poorest areas of the city to support the local church and to be closer to the growing immigrant population of the city. They were joined, a year or two later, by their niece Sylvia, a mere sixty-something. She had been a shepherd in the west of Scotland and brought her sheepdog down to Birmingham to keep her company. I remember visiting her and having a wonderful conversation when I was preparing a sermon about 'The Good Shepherd' for the very first time (how many have I preached on that theme since, and all of them influenced by that conversation!). So began my fascination with elderly people and, from that, with the process of ageing.

One of my best friends is forever saying to me, 'Don't you dread getting old? I do.' The truth is that I don't, and he most certainly does. For him, ageing is all about losing his youth and drive and vigour and vitality, though he actually lost his youth many years ago. He sees the process of growing old only as a time when all ambition fades, when his income declines, his value to society drops and he is faced by increasing problems of health and the loss of his independence. I think it was Cicero who said that life is a play with a poorly written final act, and that is certainly the view of my friend. But must it necessarily be so? Might it not be possible to have an attitudinal change which allows us to discover that ageing can be a rich and rewarding process – a time with new challenges, new heights to conquer and new discoveries to be made? In particular, might it not be a time when new dimensions of spirituality and of what it means to be human can open up?

A time of change

Much of what my friend fears is true of course. There is a loss of physical and mental strength, although we know that people age at different rates and in different ways. For most people there is a loss of income, and this is particularly true now that the world's economy is in free fall and the savings and pensions of many people have been adversely affected. With retirement many people feel that their contribution to society has also come to an end and they may have lost status and standing within the community. For many people it means that they lose their home, moving into smaller properties or into some form of residential or nursing care.

And commonly there is a diminution in their health, often quite marked and often accompanied by considerable anxiety, stress and pain.

Inevitably, there is the question of death and dying. The death of our friends, of those whom we may love, our partner, perhaps even our children, and ultimately of ourselves. Whilst death can come to us at any age and at any time, most people expect to live into their retirement years. They hope that they will die before their children, though we know only too well that this is not always the case and life does not always turn out as we would wish or plan.

So how can we be realistic about the problems and pains of ageing without being blind to its creative possibilities? Well it's never too early to start. The aged person that we may become is a continuation of the person that we now are. We carry with us into the future the attitudes and possibilities that we are now developing. This is not to suggest that radical change cannot and does not take place, but in general terms we are now creating the person we shall become. It is therefore worth giving some thought to the characteristics and outlooks which we see in the elderly people we like and respect and to reflect upon whether we can detect the seeds of such qualities within ourselves. It is never too late to develop or change, but it does get more difficult as the years go by.

Issues of health

We live at a time and within a culture which believes that, with luck, we should escape serious illness. We have built up a huge mega-system to defend us from illness and disease, from pain and from what we consider to be premature death. We have a vast array of complex drugs and the older we get the more pills we seem to need to take. Personally I am on seven a day – and that is the lowest I have been on for several years. It seems almost miraculous what drugs can achieve and for many of us our lives are transformed and enhanced by having access to them. What can't be sorted out by drugs we expect to be settled by surgery.

Today there are literally millions of people alive and living into old age who, in previous generations, would never have survived infancy, childhood, adolescence or maturity. It is truly amazing and a wonderful achievement; a remarkable testimony to people working alongside each other and sharing their skills and experience, their competence and commitment. The health services of our modern western democracies, although often much maligned, are an achievement which previous generations could not have envisaged, and which still remain far removed from the reach and experience of the vast majority of the world's population.

The corollary of such an achievement is the attitude of mind which can so easily assume that any illness which is not contained or healed somehow represents a failure; failure by a person or by a system or of humanity itself. We grow up assuming that good health is our natural right and often feel hard done by if we are one of the unfortunate people for whom medical intervention is essential, and even more so if – or when – it fails to restore us to full health. This has not been the experience of humankind over the centuries; it is a twentieth and twenty-first century and very much a western phenomenon.

How do we live with ill health or with failing health? Talking sensitively with groups of elderly people is to uncover a veritable treasure house of experience and wisdom. Within such groups are people who have come to terms with such questions, or who are actively involved in trying to come to terms with them. I never cease to be amazed by the courage and wisdom of so many elderly people, and to talk with them about their health is often to hear stories of remarkable insight, tolerance, acceptance and humour. Whilst it is true that ageing can bring for many people real problems of pain, suffering and ill health, it is also true that it offers the possibility of asking questions about life, about health and about ourselves that perhaps we have never thought of addressing. I have discovered heroes, heroines and philosophers amongst elderly people: ordinary people, people whose grasp of what is happening and whose views on life and sickness can be extremely moving and challenging. There is often a profound simplicity and gracious acceptance which stands in marked contrast to the fearful anxiety and complexity of many others who view the ageing process with profound reluctance, even denial.

Roddy was not an old man; he was only in his forties, but he had suffered. Struck down with polio as a toddler he spent his life in a wheelchair. Undaunted he moved on through school and university and toured the USA by himself as a young man in his specially adapted car. He was diagnosed with cancer less than a year after our church hosted his wonderful wedding celebration. Visiting him shortly before his death, he talked about his life. 'I never ask "Why me?",' he said. 'Such a question is like asking "Why is the grass green?", or "Why do trees grow in the way that they do?" This is who I am and this is the life I have, and I must get on and live it.'

Roddy was facing his future as he had faced his life up until now, with calmness and a clarity that was almost breathtaking. And so do many elderly people as they work away at coming to terms with their failing health and their reducing powers. There are still mountains to climb and battles to be fought as we get older, just as there were when we were young. It's just that they are different. As we grow older the invitation is to reflect upon the nature of life and the problem of pain and suffering. We are invited to explore the relationship between the length of our days and the quality of our life. It is a taxing subject, just as complicated and demanding as were those first days at school when we were much younger, but perhaps the subject matter is rather more relevant to us now.

Scaling down

One of the things that often causes anxiety as we think ahead to our later years is the fact that we may have to leave our home, perhaps the place where we have been settled for very many years and which is full of memories for us, both happy and sad. Apart from the sheer physical effort of finding a new place to live and sorting out all our belongings, there is often a feeling of guilt as though, somehow, our memories are rooted to that particular location, and consequently if we leave it we may feel that we are being unfaithful. Forward planning in regard to our living accommodation is one of the most creative things that we can do as we approach our later years. If we do it in time, then it becomes a matter of choice and we can exercise our minds (and our hearts) as to what we want and where. Far better than staying put too long and then having no choices as we are forced to move out because of illness or incapacity.

Having recently retired from active parish ministry I can see that one of the (few!) benefits of having a house tied to the job is that you *have* to move and so you can think and plan ahead about what is the appropriate space that you will be likely to be needing for the next stage of life.

Talking to elderly people within the parish who have moved to smaller and more appropriate accommodation as they grew older, I almost always discovered that their moves had been beneficial and seldom did I come across people who felt that they had made the wrong choice. There were opportunities for creative thinking and for starting out afresh, and I know many people who have revelled in such an opportunity. Moving to more appropriate accommodation can have beneficial consequences: smaller heating bills, fewer stairs to climb, less gardening to do, being nearer to a bus stop, and for many people it means that some of their capital can be realised, giving them greater choices because of extra income. As societies become more mobile perhaps people are more used to moving and the idea of staying in one house for all your adult life is becoming less of a norm.

As people move from being the younger old to becoming the older old, there may be the need to move again into more appropriate accommodation – sheltered housing, a residential home or a nursing home. If the issue of leaving the family home has been faced earlier, then it is likely that a later move is easier to accommodate. The experience of loss has been confronted and people have found that they have been able to live quite happily without many of the things that they formerly regarded as being almost of their very essence. For me, to move away and have to say good-bye to 2000 books was anticipated as a painful process. When it actually happened, I found it quite liberating. What I had been dreading wasn't nearly as bad as I had expected it to be; it's just that I had to confront the problem and work my way through it.

One of the 'in phrases' of the 1960s was 'small is beautiful'. Growing older gives us the chance to see if we really believe that. These are not easy choices that people have to make. They require considerable courage, analytical skills, determination and hope. Growing older can be just as intellectually challenging as entering into any other stage of life, and the consequences can be just as rewarding.

Recognising achievement

Western societies tend to lay a great deal of stress upon what we can achieve or have achieved: upon what we have. In that sense it is extremely materialistic. We are all caught up in this mindset whether we are high achievers or not. It is very difficult to break out of the mould. There is a tendency to judge a person by what they have achieved and by what they own rather than by who they are.

The focus of achievement is very narrow; it is defined and determined by achievers of a certain kind who have gone before and who seem to have set the agenda and the general assumptions of society. Achieving loving relationships and achieving stability or survival against all sorts of mental or physical handicaps are not taken into account. Achieving contentment, satisfaction and awareness of love and of one's own worth and acceptance is also not part of the western mindset. But these are the achievements that will last, mould and shape us and provide us with rich resources as we grow older.

There is a richness of friendship which is of equal value to richness of goods and possessions – some would say of greater value. As we grow older we shall call upon these resources more and more and we shall probably also have opportunities to replenish them. Growing older can often afford people more time for grateful reflection, for spontaneous joy and for treasuring friendships – all things which can so easily be pressurised out of the busy lives of those who are still labouring under the heat of the day.

Being grateful for our memories

One commodity that many older people have in abundance is memory, and loss of memory is one of the things which many fear most. Our memories can feed us or haunt us. We probably experience both and need to learn how to confront those that haunt us and rejoice in those that feed us. Our memories can be a huge source of contentment.

I vividly remember a 95-year-old lady giving me a wonderful account of her wedding day and how they travelled down to the south of France for their honeymoon. Her face was radiant as she told me, and she recounted how her husband had got up early each morning to go to the local bakery to bring back warm croissants. I could almost smell the bakery and it was quite clear that she delighted enormously in telling me.

Working in a parish I spent a great deal of time visiting elderly people. Many of them now lived alone because their husband or wife had died. Very often I had never known their partner; I knew them only as a single unit. I always took great pleasure in encouraging them to tell me about their husband or wife and to share with me some of the stories and incidents which had combined to make them the people that they now were. I wanted to know about them as young people: what were the things that set them alight, what were they passionate about, what had they done, where had they been. I never failed but to be wonderfully encouraged and resourced by them. What tales people have to tell, and what interesting lives!

Walking along the street with an extremely frail and almost blind elderly lady, I said that we were going to have to walk up a steep incline. 'Imagine you are in the Himalayas,' I joked. 'Oh, I used to run a hospital in the Himalayas,' she replied. I asked her if she had done any climbing whilst there. 'No, but I used to abseil,' came the reply! I never ceased to be amazed by the stories of their lives.

A lady whose funeral takes place next week as I write this told me how in the 1940s she had driven her car at over 100 miles an hour on the road from Edinburgh to Carlisle, long before we had motorways. She had been a tennis champion and travelled the world, yet when I met her she was a frail little lady with a tendency to keep falling down. But she was the same person. The outer shell had changed, her strength and vigour had almost disappeared, but how she came alive when we sat and talked through her life.

There is nothing so interesting as people, and what fascinating lives most of them seem to have led. They did not have to be high 'achievers', just growing up through the war, surviving poor housing, low wages, coping with bereavement or bearing their aches, pains and heartaches with a sense of serenity; wonderful examples of the dignity of the human spirit and the unconquerable urge to grow, learn and explore, no matter what or where it might lead. My ministry has been immeasurably enriched by the elderly people I have been alongside.

We need to find ways of encouraging people to share their memories. We need to develop the skills which can unlock these treasures (Viney 1993). One Pentecost we festooned our church with hundreds of balloons. As people came into the building you could see them stop with surprise. One man arriving early quite clearly felt that he couldn't manage such a change in his regular routine. He paused and was about to return home, but to his great credit he took a big breath and continued in through the door. Later, after the service, he was to delight with other people as they released the helium-filled balloons into the air. I had originally thought that this was something the children could do, but to my immense surprise it was the elderly folk, those in their seventies and eighties, who most enjoyed this sudden permission to play again.

> Dreams, imagination, and God's laughter in creation
> Invite me out of my industrious solemnity
> To take the task of playing seriously
> Until my marred manhood
> Is recreated in the child I have denied.

(Hare Duke 2001, p.44)

An elderly lady has been in hospital for over four years. She has dementia and is a shadow of her former self, with little communication and little apparent interest in the world around her. One winter afternoon my colleague, Mary Moffett, went to visit her and took in a box full of snow. She suddenly came alive and was overjoyed to be able to make snowballs and throw them at people in the ward. Memories were reawakened, and where to begin with there was despondency, for a moment there was joyful laughter and spontaneous creativity.

One year we decided to celebrate harvest by focusing on the harvest of our lives. Everyone was encouraged to bring items to display in church that in some way demonstrated their gifts and talents. It was a spectacular success. One lady in her upper eighties, large, overweight and moving only with difficulty, brought a tray full of medals: she had been a champion athlete in her youth, excelling over the hurdles. She looked at her display with immense pride. Another lady of 90, a pillar of society, brought large charcoal sketches of nudes. Before her marriage she had been a talented artist and had graduated from art school in the early years of the last century. The church was filled with these reminders of our human harvest and people remembered them for years.

It is often said that people only learn about other people when they go to their funeral services. How many times have people expressed amazement at the accomplishments of people they have known for years, yet so much was hidden from them? I am not arguing here for the invasion of people's privacy, but for opportunities to rejoice at appropriate times and in appropriate ways, and to rekindle memories and honour and cherish the people in our midst.

Living with our painful memories

Just as memories can be for our nourishment and growth, so they can be also for our fear and diminishment. As we age so the number of things that we have repressed or suppressed grows. Events that we may not have been able to deal with for whatever reason, which we have cast into our subconscious, may return in our later years to cause us stress and anxiety. Sometimes people cannot really be at peace until they have been able to resolve issues that were not dealt with at the time.

It can require a particularly skilled person to be able to accompany someone as they address these things. But there is still a great deal that an empathetic companion can do. Allowing people to voice their fears and anxieties, without passing any sort of judgement and without offering soft options and pious platitudes, can be a valuable resource to offer. Sharing someone's silence or accepting their tears may be more helpful than words and attempts at 'solutions'. To be alongside without any expectation of being able to understand fully or know what the outcome should or might be is a powerful gift that can be offered to a person in distress, but it is not an easy role to undertake.

> The older people who are still burdened by the consequences of earlier trauma, or dominated by the struggle to make sense of what has happened, remain in some ways victims of their experience. If they can review their experience and begin to make links between the past, the present and the future, they can move beyond being victims to take up the more positive role of survivors. To achieve this, they will have to make a painful journey through memory, feelings and intellectual understanding. (Hunt 1997, p.9)

There is often much pain associated with deaths that may have occurred a great many years ago. I know of people working through issues that occurred 70 years or more ago. There are often feelings of guilt, real or imagined, that can haunt people until their dying day. In our generation many people still feel the scars and pains of the Second World War. As we grow older we often need to reflect on the events of our life and identify the issues which have never really been satisfactorily resolved. People may need to be given 'permission' to cry, to grieve and to ask questions or display anger.

Towards reconciliation

We all have a shadow side to our being and a part of creative ageing is to have the time and opportunity to be honest about ourselves to ourselves, and perhaps (though not necessarily always) to other people. The content of our 'shadow' can be as varied as the people we are. I know of burdens carried by people, often for over 50 years or more, which include acts of unfaithfulness by the person or their spouse, an abortion during teenage years, a baby taken away for adoption, the experience of child abuse (either as perpetrator or victim), feeling guilty about the death of a loved one, feeling that a wrong choice was made in marriage (which may or may not have resulted in divorce), unfulfilled or inappropriate sexual behaviour or expression – the list is endless.

What we have here is a huge slice of human experience and pain, a desperate need for acceptance and for laying down burdens. In traditional Christian language it is similar to, but not identical with, the whole process of penitence, forgiveness, absolution and restoration.

At a much simpler level, but also important, is the opportunity that later life often gives to become reconciled with old adversaries, to reflect upon the prejudices or passions which have sometimes made it difficult to be at ease or at one with certain other people. This reminds me of the story of the two sisters-in-law who had a running feud with each other stretching over decades. After a gap of almost 20 years they met again at a family funeral. 'Goodness me,' said one to the other, 'how you have aged. I would hardly have recognised you!' Quick as a flash came the reply, 'Speak for yourself. I would never have known you if it hadn't been for that coat. It never did suit you!'

Life is too precious for us to bear grudges. As we grow older we need to make the most of the many opportunities we may have to see people in a different light, to 'bury the hatchet' and to reach a more harmonious relationship with the people around us. None of us is perfect and we all need to be generously welcomed and received.

This process of transformation is at the heart of the Gospel. We are all caught up in a process of change and we have the opportunity to influence the direction and nature of that process. Donald Nichol (1998) recounted how, as his life was drawing to an end and his battle with cancer was nearly over, he decided that, instead of grieving for lost opportunities and asking 'Why?', he would spend time each day making a list of all the things he was grateful for. He said he filled five notebooks and his days were transformed from resentment and despair to gratitude and hope. Whilst it is true that we can do this at any time in life, it seems that for many people retirement and ageing provides them with the time, space and opportunity.

Our church liturgies can provide us with a wonderful opportunity to reflect on all the good things we enjoy and have enjoyed in the past, to have time to bring our shadow to the fore within a secure environment, and to remember those who have died. In a very real sense, Christian worship can unite the past, the present and the future, and there are not many public places or events that can do that so regularly and securely.

The gift of time

I am always saddened when I hear people speak apologetically about a congregation, saying that 'it's full of old people'. I want to say something along the lines of 'how fortunate you are' because elderly people bring rich resources of experience, faith and time to the community. In a busy world, as a society which values speed becomes ever more complex and which places great demands on adults and their families, to have space and time is a wonderful gift. Elderly people have time to reflect and time to pray. We should never underestimate the contribution that they can make, even if they are housebound. They have time – a scarce commodity today. Michel Quoist (1963, pp.77–8) summed it up beautifully:

> Lord, I have time,
> I have plenty of time,
> All the time that you give me,
> The years of my life,
> The days of my years,
> The hours of my days,
> They are all mine.
> Mine to fill, quietly, calmly,
> But to fill completely, up to the brim,
> To offer them to you, that of their insipid water
> You may make a rich wine such as you made once in Cana of
> Galilee.

Looking towards the future

In order to age creatively in the present we need to be able to look backward with a sense of gratitude and forward with a sense of hope; not being sentimental or possessive of the past, nor being unrealistically optimistic about the future. There is a difference between optimism and hope. From a Christian perspective our hope for the future is grounded in the events and experiences of the past, both personal and corporate.

It is likely that as we age we shall have experiences of multiple losses. How we cope with loss, how we grieve creatively will be all-important as we move into an unknown future. Loss of hair, loss of teeth, loss of status, loss of income, loss of strength and energy – we experience loss in a thousand different minor ways, and occasionally in major and acutely painful ways. We need to prepare ourselves for loss without becoming morbid or too fearful. For most of us, it is increasingly likely that we shall develop health problems and we need to discover ways in which we face up to and endure the discomfort and possible disability that such developments may bring.

We may be confronted with long-term illness and have to make major life adjustments such as occur when people have a stroke; we may be diagnosed as having a serious illness which may or may not be terminal, and we need to discover ways of living creatively within such a scenario.

We are surrounded by people who are doing just that and we should recognise them, cherish them and rejoice with them. We may face a future that we know will threaten our identity and raise real questions about who we are, such as when a diagnosis of a form of dementia is given (Goldsmith 1996). We may be given a diagnosis which reveals that our life expectancy is short. Is it possible to find ways of living creatively when life itself is threatened? Experience suggests that it most certainly is. People with such a diagnosis are asked to face a future which is as intellectually and spiritually challenging and demanding as anything they have ever faced before.

In *Tuesdays with Morrie* (Albom 1997) a dying teacher decides that the very process of dying should be turned into his last lesson. He invites others to share the journey with him so that they can learn from his experiences and give him support and sustenance as he approaches the great unknown. In a very moving short conversation Morrie asks his former students if they would like to know what it is like. Rather mystified, they ask "Do you mean what it is like to die?", and Morrie confirms that

that is what he is means. The writer of the book then reflects that, although at the time he was unaware of it, their last lesson had just started.

It is in circumstances such as this that some people, possibly a very small minority, reach a mature judgement that they would wish their life to end and they would like to hasten that event. Voluntary euthanasia, assisted suicide, is against the law in the UK, and there are good reasons why society safeguards those who may be vulnerable. But surely there may be times when it is acceptable for a person to exercise their autonomy and we should allow them to make decisions about their own life and death? This is a difficult and complex area and not the place to argue the case, but I grow more and more persuaded that it is a subject which needs to be explored openly and compassionately.

It is at times such as these that many people discover the stars. Mysterious, far away and yet also very close, they are objects of beauty and fascination and capable of giving guidance, as mariners over the centuries have testified. The stars are always there, of course, but we only see them when the light fades and night-time comes. Surely the same can be said about many people's experience of the divine, however this might be interpreted or defined.

Is it really by sheer chance that so many people discover the resources to live creatively when outward signs would suggest that there is little to be positive about? Might it not be that, as the light fades, many people discover that there is something beyond them that they had perhaps not noticed earlier, in the brightness of their day?

The profound Christian hope is that as everything about our life diminishes and falls away, as it surely must for all of us, there remains a source of loving acceptance which takes the fragility of our nature and the multitude of compromises of our life and receives it home. Free at last, free at last, thank God almighty, we are free at last – from everything which has diminished our body, but not necessarily our spirit.

Of all the many things that I have read about death over the years, I return time and time again to these words by the German theologian Rudolf Bultmann which I discovered in a footnote:

> The man who trusts in the grace of God and who lets go all anxiety about security is also freed from all fear of death. He knows he is not the one who has to worry about his future. God takes care of it. God gives him his future and therefore God's grace encounters him even in death. We cannot

of course form any clear picture of a life after death. Yet it belongs to the radical surrender to God's grace that we renounce all pictures of a future after death and hand over everything to the grace of God who gives us what is to come. God is always the God who comes. (Bultmann, quoted in Robinson and Edwards 1963, p.138)

The stars only shine in the night: they are always there, but when we pass through times of darkness they have a habit of allowing us to see them. So, as we age creatively, relishing our new situation, looking back with gratitude, looking forward with hope, we can reflect on the present and give thanks for the gift of life.

CHAPTER 3

Successful Ageing and the Spiritual Journey

Harriet Mowat

Introduction

In Philip Pullman's trilogy *His Dark Materials* (2000) much of the plot hangs on the children's ability to identify the difference between good and evil, to relate to their spiritual selves and learn to trust these selves. Their youth temporarily protects them from some of the evils of the worlds they enter and their egos are sufficiently fluid and unformed to give them a greater sensitivity and flexibility than their adult counterparts. Their ultimate destiny however is to enter an adult world and continue their journey towards old age. One of the children is able to cut his way into other worlds, making links between them. This turns out to be dangerous work and confronts each of the central characters with his or her own mortality, morbidity and core values.

Whilst the underlying theme in Pullman's story is a rejection of God in favour of truth through storytelling, the journey into different worlds and by implication into self taken by the central characters parallels the theme that I want to explore in this chapter – the relationship between the journey into 'successful' ageing and the spiritual journey.

This chapter starts by considering the cultural and philosophical context of the emergence of spirituality, first as a legitimate topic for discussion and more recently as a legitimate area for research and intervention. It considers the rise in interest in spiritual matters in Scotland alongside the decline in religious interest, the relationship between individualism and spirituality, the dominance of evidence-based medicine and the challenge of methodology for spiritual issues, the policy mantra of patient-led services and the implications of relativism. It continues by proposing a definition of successful ageing that includes the idea of struggle and explores the anthropological universal – that of the spiritual journey. It suggests a vital and dynamic link between successful ageing and a self-conscious spiritual journey. It concludes by considering the implications of recognition of the spiritual journey from a practice and policy point of view.

Cultural and philosophical context of the emergence of spirituality as a legitimate topic for discussion

The Cartesian split of mind, body and (by implication) spirit is being challenged by a more holistic and interpretive 'turn' (Swinton 2001). The understanding of the spiritual as central to well-being is gaining currency both at an individual level, with more and more people pursuing some kind of spiritual understanding of themselves in relation to their health and well-being, and at an organisational level (Orchard 2001). The idea that health-care institutions could take on spiritual care as a legitimate part of the health-care package is increasingly seen as a reasonable proposal (Graber and Johnson 2001; Walter 1997). Spiritual care is becoming legitimised as an appropriate part of the territory of the health-care services and associated research.

One particular initiative is the work of Spirited Scotland, funded by the Scottish Executive as part of the patient-centred care focus promoted by the health minister and supported by the quality health-care division. Spirited Scotland has a remit to contribute to the discovery of the nature and scope of spiritual matters in health and social care in Scotland and to set up opportunities for health-care institutions, particularly the National Health Service, to develop spiritual policies in response to this felt need. The development of the role of the hospital chaplain is another part of this response. It is important that this newly opened territory is not prematurely fenced off and given a prescriptive methodology in an attempt to contain it.

The importance of spiritual matters to good health and well-being is a topic whose time has come. There is an increasing interest in health and spirituality, demonstrated in part by recent articles in the fields of psychiatry (Culliford 2002), medicine (Walsh *et al.* 2002), general practice (Greenhalgh 2002) and nursing (McSherry 2001). The inclusion of the topic of spirituality at conferences within all these fields is now more acceptable and in some cases expected. The British Society of Gerontology ran an entire strand on spirituality in 2001 and the Gerontological Society of America has an active and growing ageing, religion and spirituality theme and associated committee structure.

We now know that an active interest in religion and/or spirituality contributes to well-being and health (Moberg 2001). Koenig (1995) has produced an annotated bibliography relating to work done on the relationship between religion and ageing which shows positive associations between the two. However, despite these stirrings, the academic community is nervous about the topic. There are problems of definition, method and the epistemological status of belief. Whilst intuitively we feel that there must be a connection between good health and spiritual matters, the 'evidence' is hard to present in the traditional positivistic manner.

The randomised controlled trial investigating the power of prayer will always surely be a flawed study (Byrd 1988). How can we control for prayers being said for people who are in the non-intervention group? Furthermore the precise role of the variety of health and social care professionals in the delivery or response to spiritual need is unclear and debatable (Cobb and Robshaw 1998; McSherry 2001; Orchard 2001; Walter 1997). In the current context of multifaith societies and sensitivities about the dominance of any one faith, the linking of spirituality with any particular faith or with the idea of a transcendent or immanent being is also greeted with some alarm (Borg 1998).

Rise of spiritual interest and decline of religious interest

It is therefore the case that in 2003 in Scotland we find ourselves in a situation of tension and paradox in our understanding of spirituality. There is a decrease generally in religiosity (Hay and Hunt 2000). There is a decline in church attendance (Reid 2002). The populations of the churches are ageing. There is a crisis in the lack of ministers. The churches are seeking a modern role in a postmodern world.

There is at the same time a similar tension and attempt at redefinition within health and social care services where manageable definitions are sought of what it means to provide a meaningful health and social care service to individuals, where demand always outstrips supply.

There are interesting parallels in the way that both these institutions (church and health) are required to reconstruct themselves in order to meet expressed need. In the health service collaboration is promoted (evidenced currently by the 'Joint Future' initiative) on the basic assumption that it produces more coherent care for patients, despite the difficulties of finding a methodology which can show these advantages (Cable 2000). In the church there is a similar difficulty in finding a methodology which can support the intuitive belief that active interest in spirituality and religion is linked to well-being and health.

The first Scottish ecumenical conference held in Edinburgh in 2000 tried to tackle issues of collaboration between and within churches and definitions of spiritual need and service in just the same way as health and social care services are trying to tackle collaboration and definition of health need and service delivery. Things are changing and they need to change in order for the core beliefs in the power of the spirit to remain the same and be liberated as a health and well-being resource.

The decline in church attendance and religiosity has caught the attention of academics in a number of different disciplines. This is partly because other changes are taking place that are related to the *increase* in interest in spiritual matters. Whilst the religiosity of the population is declining, interest in spirituality is increasing. While our churches are emptying, our need and search for spiritual meaning apparently surges or becomes more explicit and socially acceptable, as Hay and Hunt (2000) suggests.

Interest in spiritual issues and rise of individualism

If people are expressing more spiritual need, can we be clear what this means? Is the perceived rise in spiritual awareness a misinterpretation? Has personal spirituality become confused with a rise in the interest and supremacy of the individual? Is there a confusion between the now familiar assertion of the *rights* of the individual in society and the search for self in relationship with a higher being? Individualism, which began its modern journey with the Renaissance, has now become embedded in our everyday understandings and assumptions of what it is to be human.

The general principle is that the individual has supremacy over the collective. This means that we take for granted our rights as unique and important individuals to live independent lives. It is the role of our major social institutions to support our individualism and this is enshrined in the 'policy and practice' of needs-led, person/patient-centred models of care. We are living in a world now where individual rights and needs are more and more seen as the central mechanism by which we drive our society. These two phenomena – the rise of the individual as the central focus of policy and the rise in the interest in the spiritual – are often linked together and it is important to unpack that relationship further.

The rise in individualism is linked to political expediency and philosophical and economic preference. It has been argued that individualism is yet another turn in the unfolding of capitalism since it encourages extreme narcissism which is hooked to expenditure and wealth accumulation (Ryan 2003). The search for the spirit within oneself is essentially about acceding to the will of God in order to find oneself and is a very different process from the pursuit of worldly rights and individual recognition. As we become less interested in community and 'society' (Peck 1990) and more interested in 'ourselves', so we lose one of our core meanings – that of community building. This prompts a series of existential questions about meaning, place and purpose of self.

There are clearly problems of definition of spirituality (Graber and Johnson 2001; Moberg 2001). We have to decide what we mean by spirituality as individuals, academics and health-care professionals. This is a complex area. If there is to be serious research and practice around spirituality and its relationship to ageing well, there must be an understanding of what is meant by spirituality. The definitions that we work with depend on our philosophical understanding of reality and truth. This in turn is associated with our understanding of research methods.

The research task

The lack of clarity of definition has meant that the research task in relation to spirituality is currently to establish an understanding of the spiritual as a distinct category. This, of course, immediately limits the potential of the category. The attraction of using a range of methods to investigate spiritual need and response is that it gives a much needed breadth. This is an area where the qualitative and quantitative approaches within research methods, which have become so unnecessarily polarised, have an opportunity to work together (Robson 2002).

A small longitudinal qualitative study currently being carried out by the author poses the question: 'What is successful ageing and does spirituality have anything to do with it?' The sample of older people (average age 83, n = 16) are all characterised by having had careers in medicine, nursing, social work or ministry which brought them, as younger men and women, into direct contact with older people. This gave the sample common characteristics of professional education, reflection and experience, and personal ageing experience. A number of pertinent points have come out of the extended, unstructured interviews.

The main point to emerge was a general consensus among the respondents that old age was not, of itself, of interest. Each of the respondents had a rich and unique 'journey' to report and greeted any specific questions about their experience of old age with some surprise. Their idea of success was linked to their whole life rather than their ageing process. The respondents presented themselves as 'unfolding stories', implying and asserting unfinished business and robust location of self in the present. This lent weight to the idea of a journey.

There was distinction to be made between those people in the sample who:

- had a strong faith by which they had lived their lives
- had rejected belief in God and held strong beliefs around that rejection which had influenced the direction of their lives (for instance, into a scientific career)
- didn't really know what they believed and claimed not to have give it much thought or concern.

The last group seemed the least robust in terms of the onward journey into old age, displaying doubts and concerns and less enthusiasm for the common tasks of daily life.

In a different study (Hanlon, Gilhooly and White 2002), tackling amongst other things issues concerning the relationship between spirituality and good health in later life, it was discovered, using a mixed range of methods, that there was a link between the less healthy (those who had had hospital admissions or suffered chronic disease) and the more religious (in terms of church attendance or membership). The more qualitative data suggested that philosophical uncertainty may be associated with poorer health. The advantages of this study were that both a measure of religiosity and some open-ended questions allowed a relationship to be made between measures of health and well-being and declarations of faith and religiosity. There was a matched group of healthy and unhealthy subjects which potentially gave more force to the findings. However, the problems of defining good health and poor health and the well-recorded tendency of respondents to overestimate good health may make such studies essentially flawed. This particular study assumed that successful ageing was linked at the outset to 'healthy ageing'.

Evidence-based practice and the place of spirituality

Despite the obvious value of exploring the topic across the methodological spectrum, the rise of evidence-based medicine as the gold standard upon which practice should be based, with the support of the National Institute of Clinical Evidence, and the continued dominance within that position of the randomised controlled trial as the example of best evidence, has limited the possibilities for investigating the relationship between the spiritual and health. Evidence-based medicine and evidence-based practice need definitions in order to generate evidence from which guidelines to practice can be developed.

Guidelines are part of current medical and social work practice and act as a protector for the practitioners against an ever increasingly litigious patient–client population. Following the guidelines is part of the armour for hard-pressed practitioners whilst at the same time providing ground for disagreement between professions. This perspective has its root in the biomedical tradition which assumes a positivistic and reductionist approach. There are events and phenomena which can have an effect on other events and phenomena. These can be measured using probability logic which requires big enough samples to allow statistical inferences to be made. Evidence is defined as that which can be measured.

The problem of measuring successful ageing or spiritual belief is obvious. The solution is either to leave it out or break down the phenomena and quantify that which can be quantified in order that it can be measured using a probability logic-based method of analysis. For instance, it is relatively easy to compare the rate of church attendance in relation to the presence of recorded chronic disease of a given population. This tells us nothing however of what the individual churchgoer or non-churchgoer *believes* about their spiritual lives or how they *experience* the chronic disease. It gives only a crude relationship. However, we are now in a strong position to assert that spiritual belief and religiosity do affect health positively (Graber and Johnson 2001; Moberg 2001). There have been some attempts to extend our basic knowledge about the effects of spiritual belief on health.

Evidence-based medicine and guidelines are an important mechanism by which medicine can proceed and implement its science into practice. However, it has to be taken on in parallel with the more intuitive-based practice (Greenhalgh 2002). There is a window waiting for us to step through. There is a renaissance of thinking and a general need to combine and associate two very different types of thinking. What comprises evidence must be redefined and extended.

Graber and Johnson (2001) point to some of the advantages to health-care organisations of taking on the spiritual agenda. Implicit in their thinking is the major advantage of creating an environment which hands back to individuals their relationship to God by pointing out the advantages of such a relationship, rather than becoming involved in the *delivery* of spirituality. Only the individual can actually sort out his or her relationship with God. Hospitals and health-care organisations can give permission and ensure that it is culturally acceptable to discuss these matters but it is ultimately the responsibility of the individual. Thus the organisation and particularly doctors are released from their burden of being asked to fix that which cannot be fixed. A move towards a more spiritual health service helps re-establish responsibility for self with the individual.

The needs-led culture

A further and interesting contextual factor is the emergence of the needs-led culture. This arguably is one manifestation of the individualism and independence mentioned earlier. It is a philosophical position that fits in with our times, but it also has political expediency. In the UK the introduction of community care in 1990 with the Community Care Act with its central plank of the needs-led assessment, and the current 'Joint Future' initiative, embody political, personal and bureaucratic agendas.

Of course we want to have control over our health and social care and we want the service to respond to us rather than the other way round. Needs-led service implies a rather more intuitive definitional stance. The patient or client decides in partnership with the 'carers' what the need is and by definition what the goals are and what successful completion of those goals will be.

On a daily basis practitioners confront the tension between other defined goals with implied needs and self-defined needs with implied goals. Nowhere is this more relevant than in the idea of successful ageing, defined so often as healthy ageing, with compression of morbidity into the last few years of life and physical fitness as the holy grail.

The idea of negotiated and diverse understandings of success is very well covered by Smith (1978), who notes that success depends on who you ask and who you are. This physical success of ageing (longevity and relative physical independence) must be set against the precarious journey towards interior integration and coherence, which can often only come out of adversity, disability and pain, both emotional and physical. The inevitable vicissitudes of old age offer further opportunity for growth that the march towards the goals of successful physical ageing may trample upon. Successful ageing in the internal journey sense could well be painful.

Relativism

Finally we have to consider, as part of the current context, the somewhat black hole of postmodernism and relativism. Some might unkindly argue that an appeal to relativism is an excuse not to act: it is a modern day let-out clause. Relativism opens up the door to moral blandness and gives excuses not to act on the basis of diverse experiences, an acknowledgement of individual differences. The result is a flattening of moral power and authority.

The social constructionist point of view including the negotiable nature of social life, which is the basis upon which qualitative methods proceed, is in danger of being distorted. Either it can be seen as a vehicle for endless relativism to the point where truth is utterly subjective and validated simply because it is spoken by individuals *or* it is rejected as nonsense and unresearchable, therefore dismissing the work of interpretation in which every individual engages to make sense of their world.

Social construction theory does not however negate universals. Two such universals are the ageing process and the spiritual journey. How we *experience* these universals is our own social construction and the legitimate topic of enquiry for researchers and health-care practitioners trying to respond to individual need.

Implications of this contextual backdrop for the spiritual journey and successful ageing

The re-examination of what is meant by evidence will strengthen rather than diminish the evidence-based practice approach. The inclusion of intuition is under discussion. However, we should not underestimate the power of the biomedical model to heal. The advances made in the psychiatry of old age in terms of treatment for depression and early onset dementia are examples of biomedical approaches and the careful build-up of evidence base (for instance, Lopez *et al.* 2002).

Swinton (2001) makes a powerful and readable case for a relationship between the two approaches. We now have an opportunity to re-examine health and social care needs and develop methods that give us an opportunity to tap into the less measurable facets of human need.

Negotiation of self in society *is* part of the spiritual journey. It is in this negotiation that meaning and purpose can be found. It is in the daily detail of life played out as a relationship between individuals that the spiritual journey takes form. Our responsibility as spiritual beings is to support each other on our journeys into self.

Lamb and Thomson (2001) suggest that continuity is a key part of wholeness. They suggest that continuity of self is a life task involving a number of qualitative actions of forgiveness, grace and hope. The continuity task is made easier by a discussion or conversation with significant others. For health and social care professionals interested in older people one of the tasks is to provide a setting whereby continuity of self and self in relationship with God can be maintained. One might go so far as to say that this is the key spiritual task. The I–thou discussed in some detail by

Borg (1998) and Hay and Hunt (2000) is of central importance on the spiritual journey.

The spiritual journey

We are all on a spiritual journey (Hay and Hunt 2000; Moberg 1990). For some of us religion is the vehicle or mechanism that we will choose. Others, like some of the respondents in the research described above, will utterly reject religion as part of the spiritual journey. The spiritual journey involves the search for meaning and location of self within the world and in relationship to God. Axiomatic to our humanity is our spiritual journey.

It is vital and essential to our well-being and onward movement that our spiritual journey is acknowledged. Sociologists note the dominance of such major social institutions as the family, health and social care, education, justice and church on individual lives. These institutions have an effect on our development and well-being. These institutions themselves should be able to support the spiritual journey. It is this current re-evaluation of purpose for the big social institutions that gives discussion about the spiritual an opportunity.

The idea of successful ageing

Ageing is not confined to the old. We are all ageing all the time and, whilst the imperative of reconciliation (Erikson and Erikson 1982) is more pressing in old age, the march of time makes no exceptions. Thus we are all ageing, whatever age we happen to be. We are all spiritual beings and we are all trying to be successful, integrated and reconciled individuals. Ageing and spirituality are relevant to every individual. Successful ageing is really concerned with the successful self (Bianchi 1984; Moberg 1990; Seeber 1990).

The idea of successful ageing has been influenced by the evidence-based culture. A number of forms and themes of successful ageing have been developed which put good physical health and consequent longevity at their centre and have considered the behavioural mechanisms by which these goals can be achieved, particularly the way in which individuals can optimise their existing situations. These approaches have sometimes included psychological or interactional perspectives (Moberg 2001).

If the spiritual journey is our primary task, then it becomes more pressing and vital as we age that we self-consciously engage in the journey and that we can connect with people who can help us with it.

Gerontology is multidisciplinary and aimed at understanding the ageing process. It encompasses sociology, psychology and medicine, nursing, geography, economics and politics. As a consequence there are a variety of models and 'theories' about successful ageing. The focus on the search for theory has taken a number of paths. The idea of a theory is that it should identify, explain and predict behaviour. Therefore a theory of successful ageing should be able to identify successful ageing, explain why successful ageing is present or absent in a given group and predict when successful ageing will occur. This then has the ability to offer successful ageing promotion strategies based on the theory.

There are a number of overlapping models or theories of successful ageing that are most commonly referred to in gerontology. They share some basic ideas around the presence of good health, absence of disease, evidence of independence, social activity and absence of overwhelming need.

- *Rowe and Kahn* (1997) offer us a model that strongly equates success with good health via absence of chronic disease, presence of fitness and ability to perform physical functions. Implicit is that longevity is an achievement and that compression of morbidity is a goal.

- *Baltes and Baltes* (1990) consider a behaviour-related model of adaptation and compensation. They offer seven propositions which comprise known factors associated with ageing (for instance, changes in use of memory) and this leads them to suggest that successful ageing is a process of selection optimisation and compensation. If these balances can be made then the older person can maximise their 'efficiency' in terms of conducting a normal and 'mainstream' life. They do not mention the spiritual specifically. However, they do very helpfully point out that the task of selection, compensation and optimisation is not confined to the old. Losses and gains are a feature of every decision and they discuss briefly the use of dependence as part of the adaptive process.

- *Cumming and Henry* (1961) present a model of ageing which involves disengagement or withdrawal. This comes from a functionalist perspective. This theory suggests that there is a natural withdrawal of the older person from mainstream society. In this model the clinging on to middle-aged norms and roles would be seen as inappropriate. There is an age-related functional withdrawal that allows for the smooth transition of roles from one generation to another. In this theory success is understood to be in terms of the degree of smoothness of the handing over of power from one generation to the next.

- There are psychological theories or models, in particular *Erikson and Erikson* (1982) who developed the idea that people move through psychological stages and that these are important to their journey of self. The later stages are related to reconciliation. *Antonovsky* (1987) also pursued the idea of sense of coherence as being a state of spirit that allowed one to feel content and to understand one's meaning in the world.

All these models assume a quiet movement into a different part of the life journey. Success therefore is to some extent the degree to which the movement into old age can be noiseless and untroubling to other members of society by sustaining the activities and processes of youth for as long as possible or by accepting the status of old and disengaged.

Angus and Josephine

Let us consider briefly Angus and Josephine in the context of these models.

Angus is a fit 82-year-old. He drives a comfortable car. He is well off in relative terms and can afford cruises and holidays. He plays golf three times a week with friends of his own age. He attends his local church regularly and is an active member of the congregation. He has a big garden which he enjoys and he is very sociable. He is always ready for a party. The local community in which he lives is very supportive of him and he has numerous old and established friends with whom he spends his time. His wife of 50 years died two years ago. He goes to a bereavement group set up by the hospice. When he is alone he finds motivating himself to do anything difficult. He tends to look to others to act as a stimulus. He feels that his home is somehow depleted and he is not sure where home is any more. Is Angus a successful ager? He is certainly healthy relative to his peer group, he has money and friendships. But he is desperately lonely and without continued external stimuli he becomes very depressed.

Josephine is very unfit. She is 96. She lives alone and is completely chair bound. She can't walk. She can't go out. She can't see. She has increasing urinary problems that alarm her and at the moment she deals with them herself rather than declare them. She has little money. Her neighbours are very kind and she has many visitors. She has a care manager whom she pays and who does a variety of tasks for her including her correspondence. She fears being 'taken away' into residential care. She resists being admitted into hospital and these fears make her even less mobile. Her surroundings are not very clean. She has cats that she leaves food for and she puts out food for the mice. She has a very clear and prayerful daily routine. She wakes at 5 am and prays as part of a prayer network. She also has a prayer and meditation time at 4 o'clock in the afternoon. She never misses these and asks her visitors to call at times that do not disrupt her routine. She sees her community role as bound up with her ability to pray and intercede on behalf of others. This is a lifelong view. Her cognitive abilities are intact and she says that her meditational life keeps her cognitively sharp despite her great age. If she misses her prayer times for some reason she reports becoming disorientated. She fears admission into a residential or nursing home knowing that she will not be able to maintain her personal routines.

Considering these two elders in the context of the models offered by gerontology on successful ageing it may be difficult to allocate the label 'successful ageing' to one and not the other. Angus on the face of it has a healthy lifestyle, little illness or symptoms, and is active and well off. Josephine is housebound and quietly becoming a heavy community care user and a potential 'problem' in terms of her wishes and needs being at odds with the needs of the health and social care services according to their definitions of safety and cleanliness. At the moment neither is noisy and neither is a nuisance.

Pursuing the idea that the current understanding of successful ageing is dangerously close to being ageing that doesn't become a nuisance to others, what might be said of Angus when he finds he is unable to rouse himself from his depressions? His chosen lifestyle will not tolerate withdrawal of stimuli. If the situation with neighbours and friends changes he may find himself in difficulties.

Josephine's chosen lifestyle will put her increasingly 'at risk'. If she falls and breaks her leg she will be in hospital and likely not come back to her house which requires environmental services attention.

The definition or models of ageing on offer are prescriptive and inevitably suggest an idea of unsuccessful ageing. Ageing and its discontents (Woodward 1991) can be very noisy. There may be a lot of work – the interpretive struggle for the individual on that stage of their journey may be loud and crisis ridden. Josephine will get noisy when residential care is mentioned. Angus may get noisy when he realises his bereavement is not resolvable through external activity and that he is ultimately alone.

Implications for older people of linking the spiritual journey with successful ageing

The importance and centrality of the spiritual journey must be recognised in the pursuit of successful ageing both at an empirical and theoretical level. Successful ageing must be located in the spiritual work of the individual both at a theoretical and practical level.

There seems within this to be a need to revisit the notion of dependence and independence. The idea of independence is one of the holy grails of the late twentieth and early twenty-first century and seems to be linked to individualism. It is what we aspire to in all our life stages. However, in spiritual terms independence is not the method or the goal. If we take seriously the spiritual journey as our primary task then we embark on a journey of interdependence and co-dependence with our fellows. If we can regain a more interdependent definition of independence we can start to develop a policy of mutual care and release the potential of older people to give support and comfort as well as meet their needs for support and comfort.

Finally we must make a transition from doing things to older people and wanting older people to *do* as a mark of success. We must try to move to being alongside and being in relationship with people rather than meeting targets and achieving goals. Focusing on process rather than outcome is part of the spiritual journey of successful ageing. This is a method of health and social care practice which has extraordinary power but is surprisingly absent from educational and training programmes in health and social care (MacKinlay 2001a).

Imperatives for research policy and practice

These comments are made within the working ideas of Spirited Scotland which attempts to put ideas and practice into policy initiative. There are some imperatives for research policy and practice. They imply personal and professional change and the importance of instilling confidence in health and social care professionals to take bold steps and consider spiritual issues as part of the wholistic/holistic context of health care. The mixing of the research paradigms and the production of bilingual researchers is important. This will allow the advantages and great strengths of the biomedical tradition to incorporate the anthropological perspective which gives the personal *experience* of evidence-based medicine its meaning (Robson 2002).

Research policy and practice are strange but close bedfellows. Sometimes research seems far removed from the practicalities of implementation and policy loses the research basis from which it was originally derived. By linking the idea of successful ageing with the spiritual journey and placing this relationship at the heart of the means of caring for older people we do our whole society a great service.

For further information concerning Spirited Scotland see www.spiritedscotland.org or contact the author at Division of Practical Theology, Aberdeen University.

CHAPTER 4

The Caged Bird

Thoughts on the Challenge of Living with Stroke

Penelope Wilcock

The medical scenario

Having a stroke is such a physical thing. There are so many things to be attended to medically. Of course, strokes vary – minor or major, a passing event or a huge life-changing experience – but in most cases they seem to attract the same kind of attention, the attention to physical problems. These are very pressing. Can you walk? Can you swallow? Can you talk? Can you use your hands? What medication is required?

Hospital, examinations, diagnosis, physiotherapy (the quality of this is one of the big variants), drug regime, nursing care provision, equipment – wheelchair maybe, catheter, thickeners for liquid – oh, and laxatives! Lots for carers to do. Such a physical thing. Unless you are the person who had the stroke. If you are, it can be the non-physical aspects of stroke that press in most. Depression (post-stroke depression can be very hard to shift), humiliation, loneliness, helplessness, embarrassment, frustration and the sheer aching wretchedness of loss. The word 'misery' comes to mind. It helps to talk. And of course, with stroke, you may have lost the ability to bring the words inside you out into verbal expression that can be understood.

In all life's adversities, in any misfortune, a sense of humour can be the best support and the most effective weapon. Part of the effect of post-stroke depression may well be that, just when you need it most amidst the ghastly indignities of incontinence, dribbling, clumsiness, mobility loss, your sense of humour deserts you and you haven't even the refuge of being a clown.

In terms of caring for people, my opening remarks about our tendency to focus on physical care for people living with stroke impairment may seem irritating or fatuous. *Of course* we focus on their physical care! That's what doctors and nurses and care assistants are there to do, isn't it? If we can solve the physical problems then everything else – the way the person feels – will just clear up by itself, won't it? Well, maybe.

Certainly a high standard of care and therapy, a proper diagnosis and appropriate administration of drugs are most desirable; but in any living being body and soul are not two things but one and it is simply not possible to offer effective treatment without attention to both these aspects of being. After a stroke, if a person can be helped to find their inner strength – their humour, their patience, their trust and hope and sense of self-worth – then they are in a position to maximise the therapeutic effect of their medical and nursing regime.

The factors of the spirit

Depression

This is one factor that usually has to be faced. It can and probably should be tackled medically, and recognised as a part of the pathological profile that belongs to the experience of stroke. At the same time, this very profound depression – blackness that won't shift – that often goes with stroke must be in part a natural and appropriate grief in the face of so much loss and so much adversity. Perhaps then the medical route should be just one face of a multifaceted response to the new life situation.

Equally essential might be the people – carers, ministers, counsellors, but above all else *friends* – who have the time and patience, the perseverance and the affection, to be companions on the journey of this rather terrifying road. In every adverse circumstance, to have somebody with you is the deepest consolation.

Part of every care package should be the provision of this. It is not always the case. When our relatives go into institutional care, we may be relieved to feel they will not be left at home alone. Certainly we can reasonably expect they will be washed and fed. But in many places not much more is likely to happen to them. In a nursing home, typically staffed by the minimum number of nurses and care assistants to cover the necessary provision of care, there is not a great deal of slack for just spending time with someone – and what time there is will probably go to those patients who are cheerful and positive in outlook and can speak, not to someone struggling with the overwhelming bitterness of depression who has trouble making anything understood.

To be seen and heard, respected and accepted, to have the enormity of it all acknowledged and never belittled, is perhaps a way to begin to address this profound post-stroke depression from the psycho-spiritual end.

Loss

This is of course the underlying factor in the overwhelming life experience of stroke: loss of the freedom to choose and to decide, to go out, to read, to converse; loss of personal dignity, loss of privacy. For people who have to enter residential care, this can be a very rushed and brutal way to lose their home. Loss of status and position can also be a source of acute suffering – very frightening.

A person coming into residential care is a 'patient' (a word of singularly ironic accuracy) and finds himself in a new environment surrounded by others who make the choices and decisions; who never knew him as a skilled bricklayer or a successful management consultant. He may have taken endless care and trouble digging and planting his pond or fitting his new bathroom. He may have loved pottering in the greenhouse or mending and making in his shed. He may have found deep satisfaction in sitting down at his study desk, going over his accounts, opening his emails, dealing with correspondence, starting each day by checking the full diary of a busy life. But all this will be swept away the day he goes into residential care. Who will care about anything beyond whether he's overweight and a problem to lift and move, or if his relatives have provided clothes and pyjamas that go on and off without a tussle?

It would be difficult to overestimate the impact of such deep and comprehensive loss, but it is rarely addressed. People coming into residential care are appraised not from their point of view – that has gone, maybe for ever – but from the point of view of the care staff. Will he need hoisting?

Does he have to be fed? Is he pleasant and cheerful? Does he keep ringing the bell? And, above all, before all, the eternal refrain that becomes an everyday concern, something no one ever *dreamed* of asking him until now – when did he last have his bowels open? It is hard to see how this could feel like anything less than the loss of everything.

Power

This is of importance to every human being. It is important to confidence, to a sense of self-worth and to contentment. Choosing whether to have coffee or tea, and what sort of cake to have with it, being able to go to the lavatory *now* if I wish (without help, and certainly without permission) is power. Commanding respect, impressing others with your abilities, radiating magnetism, charm and sexual attraction is power. Being able to walk out and slam the door behind me at the conclusion of a full-on fiery row is power. So is being apologised to. So is having your opinion count. Half-sitting, half-lying awkward in a chair, shirt soaked in dribble and catheter bypassing, not able to reach the bell because they forgot to put it by you when they took the lunch tray away – this is not power.

Helplessness and humiliation

Living like this brings you into daily companionship with two of the human spirit's most crushing adversaries – helplessness and humiliation. Having to wait (inevitable) contributes to this: wanting to use the toilet, ringing the bell; the staff are busy, it's not a good time (is it ever?). Eventually someone comes, looking a bit harassed, 'Yes, what is it?' The time it takes to make yourself understood. Someone else's bell is ringing, the hoist is on another floor, there isn't anyone available to help move you just right now: 'Can you hang on a bit? We'll sort you out as soon as we can.'

It's reasonable. It isn't cruel. It's just that it destroys a person's spirit – even having to ask isn't easy. All implementers of oppressive regimes understand the power to undermine the spirit and obliterate morale that lies in suffusing the satisfaction of basic human need – food, sex, excretion and autonomy – with uncertainty, insecurity and lack of privacy.

The sense of helplessness in looking at an object across the room, unable to reach or move it, in having food left on the table in front of you, not really able to manage it so some gets eaten and some gets dropped or spilt – this is crushing.

A sense of humiliation and deep shame amounting to despair can also attach to body image. A sharp dresser who favoured tailored suits and court shoes and did hair and make-up meticulously now sits awry in a wheel-chair wearing a practical tracksuit that went a bit funny in the nursing home laundry. No earrings. The essential privacy of the bathroom is lost and forgotten.

Leaks of all kinds pose a problem: eyes, nose, mouth, ears, urethra, vagina, anus – the possibilities and combinations between them hardly ever run dry! It can accumulate into a dull, hurt indifference; an unwilling-ness to be seen; a splitting-off from the self as a shameful, embarrassing thing – let go of all attempts at dignity and self-respect, surly and defiant and unco-operative, stay here in this room where no one can see.

Embarrassment

This has a considerable part to play: feeling stupid, being overlooked; what Camus used to describe as *de trop*, superfluous to the community of human belonging. The isolation and intense loneliness – bereavement – that come from the embarrassment of others. It is not easy to keep visiting someone who can no longer speak intelligibly, and whose incontinence difficulties intrude unpredictably into afternoon tea. There are so many other pressing things to do. You would have to really love that person to take the trouble to maintain the relationship.

Fear

Because of the undermining nature of depression, loss, humiliation, helplessness, isolation and shame, a further adversary of the spirit that arrives to share life is fear. This operates on a number of levels. As you struggle your way back to mobility and speech, as you meet the challenge of eating and writing Christmas cards with your left hand, as you begin all over again learning to read and speak, as you finally manage to transfer from wheelchair to lavatory – and pull your trousers down and up, and wipe your bottom – with one hand and one leg working, always at the back of your mind is the unwelcome knowledge that strokes recur. All the effort and fight and determination of rehabilitation could be unstitched in an instant; back to square one or worse. It is frightening.

There is also the fear of further loss. Maybe your home has been retained while you came into residential nursing care and you see the possibility of ever being able to manage alone there again receding further and further, so that you fear the inevitable time when you must face selling up, admitting the closure of independence, giving permission to the dismantling of that dear and familiar environment, the house of your memories, the place you were truly yourself.

On a more immediate and daily level, there are fears about physical vulnerability: the fear of falling over; the fear of continued pain and discomfort as you wait to be repositioned in your bed or chair. There are other vulnerabilities also to make you afraid: the fear of the nurse who will be on duty tonight who intensely dislikes you; the care assistant who will be with her, who is impatient and too rough, sometimes hurts you and can't seem to make you comfortable; the fear that your partner, whose visits seem more hurried, and who finds less and less to chat about, will not be able to stay the course of this grim passage. Or the fear of handing over management of your financial affairs. The fear of this going on for years is balanced against the fear of further strokes, further helplessness and death.

The carer relationship

In this daunting scenario, your relationship with your carer is thrown into sharp relief. It becomes loaded with significance. An important aspect of it is the balance of power. Humiliated, losing hope and lonely, speech, mobility and continence all shot to bits, you find yourself at the mercy of a changing procession of carers who bring a variety of different attitudes to their work.

Some of them lighten the task of your personal care with sexual innuendo, which you may or may not find amusing. All of them feel free to make the most candid observations about your weight, smell, personality, appearance and anything else that crosses their mind. Against any expectations you may until now have entertained, you learn that the invalid's chief power is helplessness; commanding attention, companionship and effecting change. Wanting, needing, demanding, whingeing and complaining become the easy and obvious route to regaining a fraction of the power and control you have lost.

Aggression and refusal to co-operate are also a means to personal inter-action; to being noticed, remembered as a person, not as an object to be processed. Two care assistants giving a bed bath can easily become engrossed in conversation and entirely ignore the person in the bed between them – but not if he might bite them or sock them on the jaw.

Ways to help

In the landscape of this rather desperate scenario, the ways to help happily are legion. They all derive from the one principle of beholding the sacred value of every living being. Before and above all else, all beings are spiritual, needy of love and worthy of respect. None of us has a magic wand that can dispel life's difficulties, and no carer can lift from a patient's shoulders the responsibility for his or her own path in life. But we can help. Anyone who has lived with or cared for someone living with stroke impairment will have found insights and strategies as good as mine – but here follow some of the possibilities I have noticed along the way.

Time

Something foundational to offer, without which the value of anything else we may bring will be much diminished, is time. Time is an increasingly precious commodity in a speeded-up world and has to be managed skilfully, all its juice extracted, nothing of its goodness thrown away. A quality of its gift is that time is not a fixed, static, inflexible thing – it is dynamic and elastic, and *timing* is as important an aspect of it as quantity. Because all of us are increasingly pressed for time in today's world, it is helpful to come into someone else's presence with a clarity about how to dance with time – make the most of our moments to achieve grace in our lives and relationships.

I am thinking that maybe a friend or relative of yours has had a stroke and you will be visiting in a nursing home; or that you are a carer and would like to do what you can to improve the sense of comfort and encour-agement for the residents where you work. Here follow four lessons about time I have been very grateful to learn.

First, here is a lesson that surprised me when I spent a year working as a chaplain in a school. Teachers are busy people. The turnaround space between the events of the day is minimal. In that setting, when an exchange of words is helpful *two minutes is adequate and five minutes is a lot*. Coming from the more leisurely pastoral encounters of parish ministry, I would never have believed it could be so, but it is. By focused thinking, by setting aside extraneous time-gobblers, by being where you said you would be when you said you would be there, two minutes is adequate and five minutes is a lot.

I have never forgotten that lesson, and it goes a long way in a nursing home. You can do a lot in two minutes – check a catheter bag, help someone to the best part of a mug of tea or a glass of orange juice, help a person blow his nose, plump up pillows, add a moment of friendly chat to the end of a routine task. Two minutes is adequate and five minutes is a lot.

If you are a care assistant, please may I let you into a preacher's secret? When a minister takes a funeral, time is of the essence. The crematorium schedule is very exact and often, if there is plenty in the way of readings, music and eulogy, time can become rather tight. It is the minister's responsibility to fit it all in without running over schedule and without making bereaved people feel the service was rushed. The way to do it is to talk fast but leave pauses. In a religious ceremony, ten seconds is a significant pause and thirty seconds is a profound silence. So three ten-second pauses and one thirty-second silence can buy you a sense of peace and reverence in the most briskly paced ritual.

It is the same with nursing care. The task of washing a patient in the evening after tea can be achieved very economically, wasting no time at all. But the minute it takes at the end of it to squeeze her hand, or give her a goodnight kiss on the forehead, or just stop and look into her eyes and say what a wonderful person she is to nurse and spend time with, is transformative.

To visit a friend in a nursing home for a leisurely two-hour chat may be an occasional possibility. To drop by with a bag of favourite sweets, a jamjar of flowers from the garden, a photo of a recent family event is far more frequently possible. Two minutes is adequate, five minutes is a lot.

The second thing I learned, from Father Tom Cullinan OSB in Liverpool, is the wonderful New Testament word *kairos*. 'Look for the *kairos*' is what Tom says. *Kairos* means both action and time – a bit like the idea of an actor's cue. As the Tao Te Ching says, 'In action, watch the timing.' It is about time as timeliness, being in the right place to do the right thing at the right moment.

This is part sensitivity, part planning. For example, if you are visiting someone who has had a stroke, it is worth knowing that the best time to visit will probably be between 10.30 and 11 o'clock in the morning. It takes a long time to get up, breakfast, wash and dress, so earlier is too early. In most nursing homes 12 to 12.30 is lunchtime. Most people who have been unwell rest in the afternoon. Teatime is early in residential care, 5 to 6 pm. Bedtimes follow quickly. The time to find someone at their best – washed, dressed, fed and not sleepy yet – is usually 10.30 to 11.00 am. To ensure that they are not embarrassed (whether or not you are) by their dishevelled, unwashed state or the aftermath of trying to feed themselves is a kindness that goes a long way.

Similarly, timeliness in conversation is important. Discussion about difficult and painful things – relinquishing financial responsibility or home ownership, for example – has to be bedded into a relaxing and leisurely initial conversation and gentled again afterwards by talk of things that comfort and restore. Timeliness. 'In action, watch the timing.' Look for the *kairos*.

Third, I am grateful to the Buddhist teacher Thich Nhat Hanh for the phrase '*looking deeply*'. He reminds us to go beyond surfaces, to use time wisely for really seeing – seeing the inner life. This may mean pondering a friend's situation imaginatively. What can I bring that is missing? A walk round the garden in a wheelchair on a warm spring day when the flowers are out? A trip to a café? Or, even better, the mitigation of enforced return to a kind of horrific infancy by that delightfully adult excursion, an evening trip to the pub?

It may mean reading a friend's silences: seeing when something is the matter, when something is achingly unsaid. Looking deeply doesn't take ages – it's like a well, not like a reservoir – it's about using moments effectively, with imagination and sensitivity. Looking deeply is a great gift, both to offer and to develop for yourself.

Fourth, the Principal of the Southwark Ordination Course where I trained for ministry, Canon Martin Baddeley, once arrested my attention by saying in a sermon, '*Jesus walked; and he stopped. What is the speed of love?*' The context of what he had to say was the gospel story of the

Syro-Phoenician woman, whose need drove her to cry out after Jesus to help her. Martin spoke about Jesus's choice of a way of being that gave him time to hear, to see and to respond.

This is a discipline of simplicity which, if we accept it, will be a gift of love to ourselves, our loved ones and all who occasionally in desperation cry out to us for our help, our compassion – our time. Jesus walked, and he stopped. What is the speed of love?

Respect

If the gift of our time is the essential prerequisite for anything else we may have to offer, another treasure we can give is respect. Part of respecting a person is giving them a *choice*. Even when someone can no longer speak or use an alphabet board or light-writer, there are many ways of discovering their preferences. It matters in simple daily things: to choose which clothes to wear today; to have alternatives from which to select a biscuit for morning coffee; to point out which of a series of photos of a beloved grandchild to send away for enlargement and framing. Offering someone a choice is a form of respect which helps rebuild self-esteem damaged by disability, and restore hope.

Respect also means at *all times* remembering in conversation and body language to include the disabled person who is present – not talking across them as if they were not there, or making decisions on their behalf without consulting them. I firmly believe that respect for a person who requires intimate care means meticulous attention to modesty, both in ensuring privacy and in the way we speak to them. Care assistants' jokes about 'just having a quick feel' or the 'harmless' jollity of sexual innuendo are absolutely out of place – even when they appear to be welcomed or enjoyed. It is inappropriate to the care relationship and therefore intensely disrespectful.

Respect also affirms and acknowledges the disabled person *as a person*. Even if they cannot speak, even if the frustration of that causes some tense and difficult moments, it restores a sense of dignity and identity to bring into conversation real interests and memories of earlier days. Sometimes we avoid these subjects of conversation because memory of what has gone can be painful and may bring a wash of grief in tears; but it is helpful, necessary, to grieve the loss of people, places, occupations we loved.

Sometimes it can be alarming when someone suffering loss of speech through stroke flies into a rage of frustration because he can't make himself understood concerning a subject he cares about – but it doesn't follow that his friends should sentence him to a lifetime of talking only about things to which he feels indifference.

Spirituality is closely entwined with identity. Spiritual care involves the affirming and rebuilding of a sense of personal identity, and the offering of respect is the means by which this is done.

Our own helplessness

It is helpful if we are to keep company with friends disabled by stroke for us to become acquainted with, and live easy with, our own helplessness. Helplessness is a very uncomfortable experience and one from which we try instinctively to distance ourselves. This can result in great loneliness for people experiencing long-term illness or disability and brings loneliness in dying, especially in a hospital environment.

People like power. They like to be able to control their circumstances. They like to be able to help others. When someone is depressed and nothing you can do will lift their spirits, when someone's speech scrambles every time they talk to you until they are glaring at you in rage as you fail consistently to understand a single word they say, when someone's need for companionship exceeds the time you have to offer until the very thought of them is enough to make you feel guilty – then the instinct is to distance yourself from them, to see them less and less. Keeping company with the long-term ill and disabled, and with the dying, can only be comfortable and sustainable if we come to terms with our own helplessness and inadequacy.

Life, death – they are bigger than we are, they just are. We won't have all the answers, haven't endless resources of unconditional love, can't always be there. We can't do everything, but we can do something. The humbling thing is that so often we come away from an encounter with a friend struggling with suffering, feeling irritable, useless and ashamed, only to learn later that just our going and spending time with him restored a level of meaning and hope.

Equanimity

Emotion, of course, is contagious. Happiness is and so is peace – but so are embarrassment and fear. It is important for us to learn how to create and maintain in good health the boundaries of our own souls, so that we do not permit our lives to be determined by the attitudes and agendas of other people.

When you keep company with someone who has recently had her life turned upside down by the indignities and infirmities of stroke impairment, it is helpful if you can maintain in peaceful awareness the attitudes you yourself have chosen: not allowing her embarrassment at the intrusion of incontinence into conversation to make you uneasy as well; not allowing the taboos around illness and death to discourage you from chatting about these things as the normal and inevitable experiences they are; enjoying the social conventions of hostess and guest, but not letting them make you feel anxious about offering to carry the tray, pour the tea or whatever is clearly going to be difficult for her. If life does not embarrass you and you are not afraid of it, your presence will relieve a great deal of unnecessary tension.

In conversation with a friend who is living with stroke impairment, as you practise looking deeply and encounter his situation imaginatively, there will be lots of things you wonder. Ask. If he has only 'yes' and 'no' or a squeeze of the hand at his disposal, explore anyway. This is not a time to pretend it all isn't happening. Be gentle. Don't be nosy. Be sensitive to the signals protecting privacy, but don't be drawn into embarrassment or fear.

Honesty

It often is helpful to acknowledge the level of difficulty and disability someone is experiencing. When you know your friend has had to give up the home she loved, it may feel dangerous ground for conversation in case she gets upset – but it's worse to have such a loss hedged about with silence and acknowledged by nobody.

When you can see your friend is struggling hopelessly with the task of putting on the stamp and sealing the envelope for you to take to the post, it helps to acknowledge the difficulty, but is respectful to leave a choice – 'Goodness me, I never thought how hard that must be to manage with one hand. Would you like me to help you, or do you prefer to finish it on your own?'

Acknowledging dread

Something that many people living with stroke impairment carry is the draining and debilitating experience of dread. At one end of the spectrum this may be associated with deep existential questions: fear of death, loss of faith or an overwhelming sense of meaninglessness. At the other end it may be fear of mundane distress: the humiliation of a bypassing catheter or of the complications of constipation – a rectum full of impacted faeces, the cramping and nausea induced by suppositories, the discomfort and indignity of manual evacuation – these can bring the dragging misery of dread.

It is helpful if you are able, without being intrusive, to enable your friend to express and explore the worst; to find, sometimes protected under layers of careful denial and turning away, where dread lies and what it is about.

Facing anger

There is a difference of opinion about anger and aggression. I have often heard people engaged in the work of spiritual care speak about someone 'full of hidden anger that needs to come out' or having 'underlying aggression'. My own feeling is that the natural state for a human being is peaceful and non-aggressive. I believe that anger and aggression are always secondary emotions, presenting when a wound still sore and raw or festering is being protected. The one experiencing it may or may not ever have the courage to expose and explore the painful place, but I think anger is rooted in pain and aggression is rooted in fear, such that confrontation or rebuke of either is non-productive. It is also worth bearing in mind that irascibility may often have a physical basis – the painful misery of pressure sores and the malaise that comes from inability to exercise, lack of fresh air and (in some people's lives) poor diet do nothing for anyone's temper.

Humour

The final tool in my box of helpful things is humour: not belittling, but softening. That which we can laugh at – with amusement, not bitterness – we have accepted and overcome.

After a time of terrifying adversity in my own life, two friends on two separate occasions said to me: 'For you to have coped with that as you did, it can only have been the strength of the Holy Spirit that carried you through.' And: 'It must have been your sense of humour that got you through all that.'

I reflected quite often on those remarks and in the end concluded that they were not only both true but that they were both the same thing. A stroke is a hell of a thing to go through – the day you can laugh about some of the indignities it brings is a healing milestone.

CHAPTER 5

The Spiritual Dimension of Ageing

Elizabeth MacKinlay

Late in 2001 in a hospital in Melbourne, I sat by my mother's bed. The evening before we had driven down from Canberra, feeling that she might not last until morning. However, this 89-year-old woman with dementia and multiple other health problems, who had made little sense in her speech for some months, responded to my voice and said, 'I've still got life in me yet!' I witnessed the defiant power of the human spirit.

The word 'spirituality' is becoming more and more widely used in western societies these days. In my field of nursing, spirituality has become so widely recognised within the past five years that there is now a chapter on spirituality and nursing in a major nursing textbook (Crisp and Taylor's adaptation of Potter and Perry 2001).

In September 2001 we launched the Centre for Ageing and Pastoral Studies in Canberra. In this new centre we are examining the spiritual dimension of ageing. We teach courses on spiritual development in later life and hope to help shape strategies for providing better quality of care for older persons.

An ageing society and quality of life

Recent years have seen enormous changes in medical technology and the ability to diagnose and treat disease and disability. Added to this, the baby boomers are also now well into their middle years of life and there are falling fertility rates in most western societies. Consequently there are increasing numbers of older people in society.

This rise in numbers of older people has seen an increase in numbers of people with dementia, with projections in Australia of a 254 per cent increase in its prevalence by 2041 (Australian Bureau of Statistics, ABS), because as people age the incidence of dementia increases. Dementia is feared by many. All the participants in a study of the spiritual dimension of older independent living people (MacKinlay 2001a), when asked if they had any fears, expressed a fear of losing control and one-third of these people spontaneously said they had a fear of getting dementia. Many had tales to tell of relatives who had become 'non-persons'. In recent research people have been reluctant to participate in the study when the word 'dementia' was used (MacKinlay, Trevitt and Hobart 2002). The term 'memory loss' however did not seem to conjure up such negative pictures for relatives or those who have dementia.

It is suggested that there is a relationship between the ageing of society and quality of life. For some years there have been predictions of approaching gloom and questions such as: Who will pay for all the old folk who no longer contribute to the workforce? What happens when the baby boomers retire? Who will pay for the increased costs of aged care? With declining birth rates, how many will be available as active members of the workforce? More recently there has been increased emphasis on retirement incomes, pension age and a general realisation that an ageing society is bringing with it new challenges and new opportunities for all to build a new kind of society where it will be a good place to live.

But we need to look with fresh eyes at who we are. We need to examine our attitudes to the value of human life and to our relationships with each other and in society. Added years to live without meaning are indeed empty years. Many of the papers presented at the Global Conference on Ageing: Maturity Matters, in Perth, Australia, in 2002, focused on these issues, with an emphasis on striving for well-being in ageing and active involvement in life.

Recent years have also witnessed rising suicide rates in older males over 85 years in Australia and the USA (Hassan 1995). An important aspect of this is the loss of meaning that may occur for some in later life. This seems to be so particularly for men. Loss of work and other roles leaves an existential vacuum. Frankl (1984) predicted this. As human beings we are essentially meaning-makers, and without meaning there remains nothing to live for. We humans are complex beings. It is always difficult to try to understand the whole by looking only at the parts. Yet, as we struggle to understand more, we need to examine the parts.

One problem during the twentieth century was the belief that we could ignore the spiritual dimension. When I started nursing in the late 1950s we were socialised into a role that clearly did not include anything to do with the spiritual, or with religion. Now I know some nurses will say that when they trained back in the 1950s or 1960s this was included in their training. Well, it was certainly not so in the mainstream of health care then. There were hospital chaplains who provided for the religious needs of patients, but the spiritual dimension of ageing had not been studied and pastoral care strategies were not well developed.

My own journey

It was only when I went to do Clinical Pastoral Education (CPE) at the end of my clergy training that the possibilities started to come together for me. Something that had been missing for me from nursing finally came into place. Even then, it was to discover the possibilities, but to realise that there was a gap in knowledge that lay between the roles of clergy/chaplains and nurses. That provided the motivation to undertake doctoral studies to examine the spiritual dimension of ageing.

Over more than a decade I have spent many hours listening to the stories of older people. This has been a privileged time, where I have learnt much and where I have been affirmed in my own spiritual journey by listening to the stories of these people.

To begin, I wanted to explore what was happening in the spiritual journeys of older people. Were they conscious of being on a journey and, if so, what was it like? What were the possibilities? Was there hope yet in growing older and more frail? It was vital to allow the older people to tell their own stories, rather than to impose the structure of a questionnaire on them that might not ask the questions which were important to them.

I began my studies formally with my doctoral work in which I examined the spiritual dimension for a number of older adults, all more than 65 years of age and living independently in the community. I used grounded theory for my research methodology (Annells 1996; Glaser 1978; Glaser and Strauss 1967), employing in-depth interviews which were taperecorded, transcribed and examined for themes.

Since completing my doctoral studies I have returned to listen to the stories of frail older adults resident in aged care facilities and have built up a picture of the spiritual dimension amongst cognitively intact older adults. For my latest research, with a Linkage grant (ARC) awarded for 2002–4, I am seeking to extend this to the spiritual dimension of people who have dementia. In total, by mid-2002, I had conducted in-depth interviews with about 70 older people, gradually building the picture of spirituality in ageing.

I am suggesting that the beginning of this twenty-first century is an important time to reflect on what spirituality is, and how far we have come in fleshing out the bones of this dimension which was so much neglected during the twentieth century. This is also an important time to vision and plan for the future as we face global ageing, with both the opportunities and challenges that it brings.

The way we handle issues of ageing and spirituality now will be critical to our well-being into the years that lie ahead during the course of this century. The issues strike to the heart of what it is to be human. In this chapter I want to explore this dimension of being human – the spiritual dimension.

So what is this thing called 'spirituality'?

It is necessary first to differentiate between religiosity and spirituality. Until recently there was no evidence to support the effectiveness of spiritual care or pastoral support. Most earlier studies had simply looked at church attendance; that is, they had measured evidence of religious behaviour (Harris 1990; Kaldor 1987). It is certainly easier to measure these things. But now research is advancing quickly in this new field (Kimble *et al.* 1995; Koenig 1994).

However, a word of caution is needed here. Care must be taken not to use spiritual strategies like pills that can be taken to cure a condition. It is important to check directions in research continually to see that integrity in research design and methods is retained and that the type of research is appropriate for the topic to be studied. We are not after a 'quick fix' but rather looking at issues that lie at the heart of what it is to be human.

Research must be closely linked with the experience of life for older people. This is the direction taken in a current research project in which I am involved, titled: 'Finding Meaning in the Experience of Dementia: The Place of Spiritual Reminiscence Work' (MacKinlay, Trevitt and Coady 2002–4). In this project university faculty members work closely with aged care industry partners.

A definition of spirituality

There is a great deal of discussion as to the definition of spirituality and many variations are offered within the chapters of this book. Some may argue that it is not possible to agree on any one definition. Yet it seems important to attempt to identify both the field of practice and the parameters of study if this dimension of being human is to be developed at all. It is a prerequisite to recognise at all times the human being as having physical, psychosocial and spiritual dimensions. The definition I have used in both my main studies is:

> That which lies at the core of each person's being, an essential dimension which brings meaning to life. It is acknowledged that spirituality is not constituted only by religious practices, but must be understood more broadly, as relationship with God, however God or ultimate meaning is perceived by the person, and in relationship with other people. (MacKinlay 2001a, p.52)

Thus, the spiritual dimension is recognised as that which lies at the core of one's being. I am suggesting that this is a generic concept, in that each person has a spiritual dimension which is worked out in that person's sense of deepest meaning in life. It is from this core of existence, perhaps more properly called the soul, that people respond to life. It is what gets people up in the morning, what they would live or die for; it is what motivates and it is what brings them hope.

As every person has a physical and psychosocial dimension, so they also have a spiritual dimension. As with the other dimensions, some of us have well-developed spiritual dimensions, others of us may have few spiritual resources. So, each of us has a spiritual dimension, but the way we work out our individual spiritual lives differs from one person to another. This is our specific spirituality.

Core meaning

Spirituality involves relationship with God and/or others. For some, deepest or core meaning in life comes from relationship with God. For numbers of people, relationship with other people is the source of greatest meaning in their lives. For some, core meaning may be derived from work, from the arts, from the environment (MacKinlay 2001a). Worship, prayer and other religious activities form an important part of response to meaning, and form a part of spirituality for large numbers of older people. In *The Spiritual Dimension of Ageing* I outlined a model of spiritual tasks of ageing that was based on the stories and data collected from older independent living people (MacKinlay 2001a).

Each person has the task of finding ultimate life meaning for themselves. However, meaning is not made, but rather it is discovered (Kimble *et al.* 1995). In workshops conducted with nursing home staff (MacKinlay 2001b) they grappled with the questions: What brings greatest meaning to my life? What gives me energy for living? Why am I here? It seems important to assist those who work with older people to explore their own spiritual dimension before they assist those they care for.

For many older people in my studies, the answer to what brings greatest meaning for them has been through relationship with others, most often with spouse if they have one, then with children and/or grandchildren (MacKinlay 2001a).

In my research of the spiritual dimension in later life I found a change in emphasis from the independent living group to the frail older nursing home residents as to where they found central or ultimate meaning. The frailer older people were more likely to say that God – and for Christians that Jesus – was the centre of their lives (MacKinlay 2001c). For those living independently, other human relationships seemed more often to be at the centre of their lives.

Assessing spiritual needs in the light of ultimate life meaning

Assessing what lies at the core of one's life is important, both for older people and for those who provide care. First, those who provide care must begin their care from a sense of self-awareness, so that they do not project their own beliefs and values onto another. It is only by being aware of one's own spirituality that one can meet others where they are.

Second, what brings greatest meaning to each individual is the starting point for that person: it is from this point that they respond to life. Thus the challenge for the care provider is to connect with the person and listen to hear where that individual is spiritually. For example, if the person has an image of a judgemental God, then guilt may be a central feature of their lives and they may not be able to see hope in their present situation. If the person has an image of a distant God or god who does not intervene in human events, that person will not see any possibility of help or strength from that source. On the other hand, if the individual has a relationship with a God they see as loving and close to them, this may provide a positive approach to well-being (MacKinlay 2001c).

If core meaning comes through relationship with loved ones, it is important to know this, especially if a central relationship has been lost through death. It may be that core meaning has come from work (although in fact none of the independent living people I interviewed derived their greatest meaning from work) and that role is now lost for many in retirement.

Ongoing assessment is necessary to raise staff awareness of the current spiritual needs of each individual and this relies on those who work with older people being able to recognise that people do have a spiritual dimension and not making assumptions as to what shape that may take.

Response to ultimate meaning

People respond to what lies at the core of their being, what is most important in their lives. In my studies, a range of responses was found. The single most significant source of meaning was through relationship and this is discussed later in this chapter. Where art, music or environment formed central sources of meaning, then the person would respond to meaning through these. If God was central in providing central meaning, then for Christians worship, prayer, reading of sacred scriptures, or meditation may be means of response. For those in the study (MacKinlay 2001a) who followed Buddhist teachings, meditation was an important part of their response to meaning.

If loss of ultimate meaning was predominant for a person, then it may be hard for that person to find any response to meaning. This is a factor in grief and in depression.

Both developmental and situational crises may throw up issues of life meaning for the individual, and hence be a stimulus for a repositioning of life meaning. This in turn would call for a new response to new life meaning.

Human beings are by nature meaning-makers in that they seek for meaning in the everyday situations in their lives. People use symbols and ritual to represent meaning. Good ritual connects deeply with the soul. It illuminates meaning for the individual and also represents shared meaning within a group of people (MacKinlay 2001a). In Alzheimer's disease the use of symbol and ritual remain important because people who have cognitive disabilities are still able to respond to liturgy emotionally, and in this way, through Christian liturgy, they can still be part of the Body of Christ.

Self-sufficiency versus vulnerability: self-transcendence

An important theme from both independent living older people and residents in aged care was that of self-sufficiency versus vulnerability. In western societies in the twentieth century self-sufficiency was highly regarded, and the push for individualism promoted (Bellah *et al.* 1985). However, we can never be truly autonomous individuals for we each need others at some point in our lives. We are in reality interdependent, we need community.

'Betty' (the name I use for her), one of my independent participants, said, 'Oh, we're all afraid of dependence.' She spoke of a friend who has Alzheimer's and of her fear of getting it. 'This is you know, half a person in a sense, so I've seen that happening…just only beginning and if that accelerates I think it will be a big fear, partly dependence, partly you're losing yourself aren't you?' (MacKinlay 2001a, p.150).

This is a common fear of Alzheimer's disease, but there is a sense in which it is not so much a loss of self as an inability to communicate what is yourself to others.

Wisdom, storytelling and final meanings

In recent years wisdom has been examined from a psychological viewpoint (Baltes and Baltes 1990; Blanchard-Fields and Norris 1995; Sternberg 1990; Thomson 2001). However, it is necessary to look at wisdom from beyond the psychological paradigm. The psychological, with its emphasis on cognitive structure, falls down in the process of frail ageing and the decline of cognitive function in dementia. Is it simply a cruel joke that would see the crowning of one's years with the loss of everything that one once held dear: intelligence, wisdom, memory? Is that all there is? Christine Boden, who has fronto-temporal dementia and is author of *Who Will I Be When I Die?* (1998), has spoken of those of us who do not have Alzheimer's as being 'TABs, temporarily advantaged brains'.

One of the spiritual tasks of later life is to tell our story, in the context of approaching the last career of life, preparing to die. This is where we can come to know the final meaning of our lives. As we age there is the possibility to reminisce, to go back over life and affirm, reframe, to see who we really are in the light of all that we have been and have experienced and learned throughout our lives.

It seems that for most people reminiscence is a naturally occurring activity, part of handing on our part in the cycle of the whole of humanity. There is too still that openness to the rest of our lives, the part not yet lived and the hope inherent in those last times. Erikson wrote that the task of this final part of the life cycle was the struggle between integrity and despair (Erikson, Erikson and Kivnick 1986).

If this final part of the life cycle, the last career (Heinz 1994), is successfully negotiated then the move is towards wisdom. Thus wisdom is more than cognitive. It is suggested that wisdom, to be understood fully, must take account of both the psychological and spiritual dimensions. Thus, for wisdom in later life, a spiritual view is proposed: 'An increased tolerance to uncertainty, a deepening search for meaning in life, including an awareness of the paradoxical and contradictory nature of reality; it involves transcendence of uncertainty and a move from external to internal regulation' (MacKinlay 2001a, p.153, based on Blanchard-Fields and Norris 1995, p.108).

Edith was one of the participants in the study of independent living older people (MacKinlay 2001a). She had only attended two years' high school and was at the time of the interview nearly 80 years of age. Following a cardiac arrest she asked why she had been brought back to life. Edith answered her own question, remarking that she used to be full of anger and that she thought God didn't want her to 'go out' like that.

She wrote the following poem that illustrates so well the spiritual component of wisdom in later life; the ability to live with ambiguity, with uncertainty, to transcend her difficulties, to ask questions of her life and to seek for meaning in them:

> 'Tis fear that I'm really afraid of,
> that I'll not be able to conceal it
> and I'll show my shame to all
> I would like to live a little longer,
> to see my grandsons grow taller
> please Lord, grant me courage to face it well
> let me laugh when I feel like screaming loud
> let me think of those who gave a helping hand
> and let me cast out the anger I had
> at those who hurt me through the pages of life
> anger, fears, and contempt
> why did I let these thoughts twist my mind?
> they only destroy the good within us all
> we can change these thoughts
> for God is still there within our soul

(MacKinlay 2001a, pp.173–4)

Relationship and isolation

The need for intimacy in later life

Intimacy is just as important in later life as at any time along the lifespan; perhaps even more so in the frailty of later life where, having lost physical or cognitive abilities, the person is even more in need of relationship and love. So how are we to understand intimacy? Carroll and Dyckman (1986, p.123) write: 'At the deepest core of my being I need to be known and loved as I am.'

Studies of independent living older people (MacKinlay 2001a) have found that the most important source of meaning in the lives of the majority of informants came from relationships: with partners, if they had them, and from children and grandchildren. For a number, these relationships provided the reason for living: that is, relationship provided core meaning. Residents in aged care facilities are even more likely to be frail and to have experienced major losses in life, such as loss of their spouse/partner. They have then lost their place of residence on entering the home, and sometimes even their identity.

Often there is no one to speak to about their losses and their fears and no one to share intimacy with (MacKinlay 2001c). Human beings need intimacy, in later life as at any time during the lifespan. Just as infants and toddlers who are deprived of love fail to thrive, frail elderly individuals too may be deprived of nourishment of the soul and may also fail to thrive. Some in residential care may only experience the touch of another human in the feeding, showering or other caring activities, but never simply as an act of love.

The importance of hope

The human spirit is nourished by and flourishes on hope. To find hope is one of the spiritual tasks of ageing, although of course this is not a task for older people only. In the study of independent older people (MacKinlay 1998), hope for many of the participants was tied to seeing their children well established in adult life and their grandchildren doing well. I did not specifically ask questions of hope and belief in life after death as the in-depth method of questioning focused on issues that the participants raised within a broad framework of questions. However, few of the independent older people spoke of eternal life, although some widows spoke of hoping to be reunited with their husbands.

Constructing a model of the spiritual tasks of ageing

The themes discussed above were all derived from the data of transcribed in-depth interviews of older people. The themes were based on their stories; these themes were *their* themes: what they saw as important and relevant to their lives, not what the researcher saw as important. The themes from the interviews were:

- ultimate life meaning
- response to meaning
- self-sufficiency versus vulnerability
- meaning and wisdom in later life
- relationship versus isolation
- hope versus fear.

The themes were analysed and a model of the spiritual tasks of ageing was constructed based upon them. This model is a dynamic one with interactions between the themes named above which are all related to the ultimate life meaning at the core of each person's being. Depending on where the individual finds ultimate meaning, they will respond to that meaning in ways that are appropriate for them. Further, there are interactions with the other four themes of self-sufficiency versus vulnerability, finding meaning and wisdom in later life, relationship versus isolation, and hope versus fear. The tasks are then linked to the themes:

1. From the theme *ultimate meaning* came the task to search for ultimate meaning in life.

2. From the theme *response to ultimate meaning* came the task to find appropriate ways to respond to meaning. Obviously the ways of responding to ultimate meaning will be based on what the individuals see as being of most importance in their own lives.

3. The theme of *self-sufficiency versus vulnerability* became the task to search for transcendence.

4. The theme of *meaning and wisdom* became the task to move and search from provisional to final life meanings.

5. *Relationship versus isolation* became the search for intimacy with God and/or others in the face of loss of long-term relationships.

6. For the theme of *hope versus fear* the task became the search for hope.

These spiritual tasks are illustrated in Figure 5.1. The tasks we have identified are not to be understood as jobs to be done and completed, but rather as a process through which an individual may move, the process always being dynamic: maybe at times going back to revisit earlier experiences of life (reminiscence), perhaps reframing the meanings of these experiences, while at other times moving onwards. Different life experiences may stimulate further movement and development in the tasks. People will be at different points along the way to achievement. The tasks may not be completed in this life, but have the potential to continue at least to the point of death.

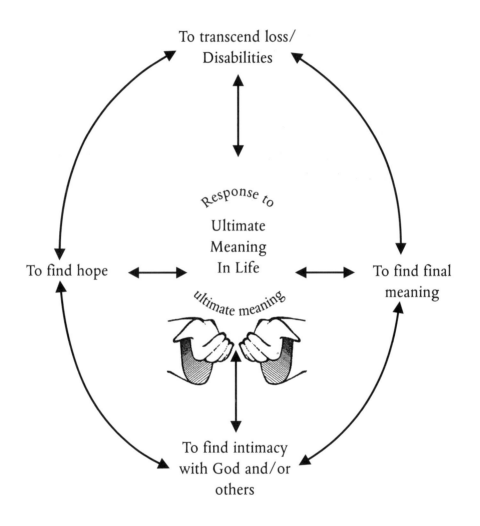

Figure 5.1 The spiritual tasks of ageing
Source: MacKinlay (2001a, p.224)

Conclusion

This research process of listening to the stories of older people and seeking to map the spiritual dimension has been a time of privilege, through which I as researcher have heard the unique stories of so many people. On so many occasions the people involved have thanked me for listening to them, yet I do believe that it has been special time for me too. At times during the interview process, the whole interaction became sacred space, where the person shared deeply of the things that were most important to them. It was truly a privilege to be present as they unfolded their life stories before me.

We still have much to learn of the spiritual dimension. It is now becoming evident that what is known as 'narrative gerontology' has an important part to play in the continuing of our societies, the affirming of our older people and the beginning journeys of the younger ones in society. Yet it is not simply telling the story as a pastime for older people that is important, but at a much deeper level it is engaging with the meaning of life itself that lies at the base of this enterprise.

CHAPTER 6

Ageing and the Trinity
Holey, Wholly, Holy?

Rosalie Hudson

What does it mean to explore the themes of ageing, spirituality and well-being within the ancient Christian liturgical framework of the Holy Trinity and the thrice-repeated litany 'holy, holy, holy'? In this chapter the contemporary gloss – 'holey', 'wholly', 'holy' – is used as a means of uncovering and examining the meaning of ageing in contemporary society.

After peering into some of the 'holes', contrasting views of spirituality are offered as they impact on ageing 'wholly'. The third stanza of the litany shows that to be 'holy' is to acknowledge the dialectic of ageing and to become part of the narrative. Finally, a brief excursus into Trinitarian theology will emphasise the profoundly interpersonal nature of Father, Son and Holy Spirit who invite us into the conversation and the musical harmony of loving, reciprocal relationships, not for God's sake but for our own.

Holey

In exploring the first 'holey', gaps are identified in some care practices that raise questions of our claims to 'holistic' ('wholistic') care. Is our care for older persons, particularly those requiring 24-hour, long-term care, really holistic or hole-free? With an increasing emphasis on diagnosing disease and treating physical symptoms, are some of the psychological and sociological aspects of care left unattended? In our emphasis on tasks to be performed, are there holes in our care that allow matters of the spirit to slip through unacknowledged? What does it mean for the older person's well-being, and our own, when these issues are ignored?

Fragmentation

There is a tendency among carers to use the word 'holism' in reference to the body–mind–spirit, and to imply that they are practising holism if they administer a bed bath and give medications (body), refer the patient to a psychotherapist or social worker to sort out their problems (mind) and ask about the patient's religious preference and call a vicar, priest or minister as appropriate (spirit) (Wright and Sayre-Adams 2000, p.4).

In this analysis Wright points beyond a fragmented or holey frame-work to a different concept of holism, where each human person is viewed not as an amalgam of parts but as an interconnected whole. Moreover, as the emphasis of this chapter will show, each person is seen to be interconnected with every other person, none of us existing in isolation. Therefore, there are holes in our care when we divide a person into parts or when we separate them from their network of relations; more particularly when we separate ourselves as 'carers' from those who are 'in need of care'. As Henri Nouwen says:

> Only when we are able to receive the elderly as our teachers will it be possible to offer the help they are looking for. As long as we continue to divide the world into the strong and the weak, the helpers and the helped, the givers and the receivers, the independent and the dependent, real care will not be possible, because then we keep broadening the dividing lines that caused the suffering of the elderly in the first place. (Nouwen and Gaffney 1976, p.153)

Conversely, when we lessen the dividing lines between those who are perceived to be the stronger and those perceived to be the weaker, then we may influence the closing of the gaps and the transformation from 'holey' to holistic. In this way, says Nouwen, we 'allow the elderly to cure us of our separatist tendencies and bring us into a closer and more intimate contact with our own aging' (Nouwen and Gaffney 1976, p.18).

Bio-medical paradigm

Further exploration of this term 'holey' reveals in the contemporary 'spirit of the age' a number of flaws or holes that suppress the true 'spirit of ageing' (Hudson 2003). Much of the emphasis in the 'spirit of the age' is on youthful vitality, physical perfection and denial of the ageing process. In a cultural milieu that prizes perfection over defects, fitness over frailty, youth over old age, we have generated 'a particular glorification of youthfulness and an irrational denial of the natural life processes of ageing and dying' (Kimble 2001, p.32).

Furthermore, says Kimble: 'The bio-medical paradigm is not hermeneutically nor philosophically equipped to explore and create new dimensions for understanding the meaning of growing and being old' (2001, p.33). Similarly, Seeber asks: 'Why shouldn't gerontology lead the academic enterprise away from the ever-splintering precipice of enquiry toward a more wholistic and perhaps more rigorous anthropology and theology of life?' (Seeber 1990, p.3). There is a growing awareness that an exclusive focus on empirical science is not sufficient to cover issues of life's meaning as we age. There are gaping holes in this view of the world, particularly a world where the numbers of older people are increasing so rapidly and all we offer in response is the prediction of an economic blow-out or 'tidal wave' (Hudson 2000).

Taking up this oceanic metaphor, we may address the question more profitably by enabling older people, including ourselves, to turn the tide with hope and confidence of reaching a safe shore. Choosing a different current we swim together, supporting each other with a buoyancy founded on shared experience. In other words, what is needed is not more statistics or mere statistics but understanding, not more information about diagnosis and prognosis but more enquiry into the meaning of ageing. This search for meaning is a spiritual exercise involving us all at every stage of our lives, a point reiterated in the final section of the chapter.

Quantification

According to the spirit of the age, important criteria for measuring ageing are quantifiable factors such as productivity, lucidity, capacity and physical perfection. Where are the holes in this analysis? Max Weber (1976) warned that we're creating 'specialists without spirit, sensualists without heart', and so we delude ourselves that we're attaining a new age of civilisation. In the spirit of this 'new age of civilisation' one of the holes or flaws is an understanding of spirituality that takes seriously a meeting of older people at the heart of their experience. According to Weber's analysis, the tools of the aged are not effective for filling this gap. Like the bucket in the 'dear Liza' song, have we no alternative than to try to mend the hole via the circuitous route of using the straw that needs cutting with the knife that needs sharpening with the stone that needs wetting with the water the bucket can't carry because there's a hole in it?

Autonomy

Harry Moody identifies another of these holes, as he casts a critical eye over the 'holy god' of autonomy:

> The irony is that we want to uphold autonomy for the elderly at just the time when their condition makes autonomy least attainable, and at a time in life when other human needs – for care, for respect, for meaning – are more pressing. Yet the poverty of our moral discourse is such that we can only offer to those in the last stage of life *more autonomy*. (Moody 1992, p.4)

This concept of autonomy presumes that what older people need is more self-directed decision making, leading to greater freedom and independence. As Moody points out, in bowing to the holy god of autonomy, issues of relationships with others are ignored. When the emphasis is on *inter*dependence rather than independence, freedom derives from shared goals and from helping each other achieve meaning as we age. Concentrating only on autonomy and individual rights, we remain aloof from each other and the hole becomes a deep chasm.

Privatised individualism

As well as the holy (or holey) god of autonomy, the spirit of the age is characterised by the holey god of privatised individualism. This god assumes each person has the inalienable right and ability to select freely their own path through life without reference to others. Spirituality, according to this spirit of the age, is then directed inwards, with no reference to any transcendent influence. In the current discussion, however, spirituality is understood to come from a different source, leading towards a different goal.

Spiritualitas comes from the fifth century, 'referring to the quality of life which should result from spiritual gifts imparted to all who believe in Christ' (Cross 1997, p.1532). In other words, from a Christian perspective, the spirit of spirituality comes, not from individualised self-fulfilment or privatised religion, but from a source outside ourselves. This spirit is for sharing with others; fulfilment comes only through forgetting oneself, giving oneself, focusing outside one's self. Kimble writes with conviction:

> The Christian religion with its historic perspective on the cumulative resources of the spirit sets forth affirmations and principles that help individuals and the community of faith confront the human aging process in all of its bewildering ambiguity. (Kimble 2000, p.142)

To acknowledge a transcendent perspective on life is, according to Kimble, neither 'escapist nor evasive'; we are encouraged to face squarely and in the company of others the mystery and ambiguity of ageing.

All in the mind?

On the other hand the spirit of the age is characterised by a seductive invitation to well-being through independence, bodily perfection and agelessness. The pimple-free obsession of our youth has become the wrinkle-free obsession of old age. We have been tempted towards the promised land of a new leisure society heralded by unimagined freedom brought about by early retirement and a lifetime of creative and artistic pursuits punctuated by stimulating sports and relaxing pastimes. If this is not achieved, then we are encouraged, particularly by the media, to mend the flaws in our lives. The media would thus have us believe ageing is all in the mind. With a few self-help books here, a little cosmetic surgery there, concentrating on creative leisure pursuits – bungee jumping at 103, popping a few pills of promise along the way – we are, according to a recent article in the Melbourne *Age*, rapidly accomplishing 'the death of ageing'. The authors claim that 'old age is now withering with dizzying speed' (Szego and Milburn 2002, p.5).

To reify ageing in this way is to enslave it, to perpetuate an entirely illusory attitude, claims Richard Neuhaus as he describes a new book that recently came across his desk:

It offers a program for 'total well-being' – physical, mental, spiritual – along with elaborate guidelines for workout routines, diets, and 'totally there' sex. It sounds utterly exhausting in its reach for the superfluous and neglect of the necessary, and the possible. (Neuhaus 2001, p.82)

This is not to take a stance against well-being in every area of life or to deny the importance of healthy ageing in all its manifestations. What is needed, however, is a realistic perspective on what is necessary and what is possible. In much advertising, and in many government pronouncements, ageing is presented with a self-congratulatory smugness that denies the existential reality – that old age may be characterised both by exhilaration and alienating depression, by remarkable productivity and total dependency.

True spirit of ageing

This unrealistic 'spirit of the age' fails to illuminate the true 'spirit of ageing'. The enemies of the 'spirit of the age' are dependence, imperfection and degeneration, regarded as flaws to be covered up, problems to be solved, and ultimately a burden too great for society to bear. The 'spirit of ageing' is, however, one that engages us in all the vicissitudes of life, but our language stumbles as it tries, against the power of positive thinking, to capture this paradoxical amalgam of joy and pain, pleasure and suffering. Michael Ignatieff, in his powerful commentary on *The Needs of Strangers*, says:

> Needs which lack a language adequate to their expression do not simply pass out of speech: they may cease to be felt. The generations that have grown up without even hearing the language of religion may not feel the slightest glimmer of religious need... Words like fraternity, belonging and community are so soaked with nostalgia and utopianism that they are very nearly useless as guides to the real possibilities of solidarity in modern society...our language stumbles behind like an overburdened porter with a mountain of old cases. (Ignatieff 1984, p.138)

Ignatieff further suggests the state of our spirit is such that we believe meaning can be established only in the private realm of our individual existence, rejecting the need for 'any collective cosmology or teleology' (Ignatieff 1984, p.78). What language do we have for matters of the spirit, of the heart, of the soul? Where is our vocabulary for the nurture and growth of the self over a whole lifetime? Where is the discourse for enunciating the purpose of our creation and the end to which we are called? How may we learn again to *feel* the needs articulated by so many who require care?

The language of the age is captured in the icons of 'drive-through surgery' or the quick fix, technological wizardry, case management, short-term contracts, throughputs and outcomes. There is little place for words like faithfulness, commitment, interdependency, interrelationships, service, love, hope and long-term care. And yet long-term care will be required for many whose increased life expectancy may also include the processes of chronic disease. Aged care is no longer the transient short-lived affair of the postmodern hospital; it is the committed long-term relationship that requires holistic care and, for better or worse, faithfulness to the end.

Dementia

One of the greatest challenges for holistic care comes from the person with dementia. With the increasing prevalence of dementia there are not many of us who will forever remain untouched in some way by this mysterious malady. Here also is a challenge to our language: 'He's lost the plot.' 'She's no longer the person I knew.' 'It's like a living death.' 'I couldn't bear to finish up like that!' What discourse is needed for engaging with those who are inarticulate or whose spoken words are unintelligible to the hearer? How do we describe our relationship with a person who appears unable to respond to us in any meaningful way? Jackie Treetops (1996) provided a very practical guide to relating to and tapping into the stories of people with dementia.

Thinking seriously about the issue of dementia in relation to this discussion on ageing and well-being prompts further questions. What is the source of our humanity? Do we become less human if we are no longer able to remember our name? What is the source of our spirituality? What does it mean to be wholly human?

Wholly

The second part of the litany calls for a consideration of what it means to age wholly. Rowan Williams says that in order to be whole we need a faithful presence to hear our story: 'I have no reality as a subject that is not also a reality for and in another subject' (Williams 2000a, p.166). Such faithful presence requires us to recapture the lost skill of 'attentive stillness which is somehow bound up with *being* attended to' (p.175). It seems therefore that ageing wholly and caring wholly are indistinguishable. We age wholly and care wholly when we enter the narrative of the other person. Caring in this context takes on a different pattern; it is more than 'doing to', nor is it merely 'being with'; a faithful presence involves not only our attention but our being.

Mutuality and reciprocity

To ask where spirituality fits into ageing and well-being is also to focus on mutuality and reciprocal relationships rather than, for example, ascertaining objective data for an assessment sheet. In entering the narrative, a carer may indeed identify the older person's feelings: their fears, their anxieties, their dreams and their hopes. In response, the attentive carer will not merely tick boxes on a form. The point at issue is that even the most comprehensive spirituality assessment tool may not treat persons as whole, but may further divide them into parts, particularly when specific forms of documentation are produced solely for bureaucratic purposes such as the auditor's visit.

By contrast, the attitude of the attentive carer will inspire confidence and trust that these deeply spiritual issues will be heard; and not only heard, but responded to with love and reassurance. Spirituality is not merely one dimension of a person. Spirituality lives and flourishes in the way we care for one another (Walter 1997).

The essence of spiritual care is the sharing of a story and in this dialogue we are equal partners. We come not with answers but with ourselves. To return again to the 'dear Liza song', we don't fob off the person by going to get the straw that then has to be cut with the knife that has to be sharpened by the stone that needs wetting with the water we can't carry because of the hole in the bucket. Rather than the plaintive, pathetic cry 'There's a hole in my bucket, dear Liza', we may say in effect, 'I don't claim to fully understand what's on your mind and in your heart. I don't have clear answers to life's questions myself, but I will stop, I will sit beside you and *attend* with my *being* to your story.'

Meaning of ageing

Viewed from within this framework of mutuality and reciprocity, the question of ageing and well-being is too great a responsibility to leave to biologists, physicians, gerontologists, sociologists, psychologists, economists, geneticists or demographers. Rather than an exclusive focus on empirical science, we need the everyday stories and wisdom of one another to provide a broader understanding of these issues. What does it mean to live together in this age or that age?

This frame of reference asks not what we should *do* about the ageing *problem* but what is the *meaning* of ageing. This starting point would then look for different resources. What resources are given to people who attend retirement seminars, even those run by the church? Most common are resources that focus on financial planning, or how to fill every day with busy-ness and new challenges. Rather, questions that focus on ageing wholly may take a different course. What will nourish me, what will I need to sustain me as I grow older, to give my life meaning not merely as an old person but as a citizen; not as an isolated individual but as a person in community with others? Who will nourish me, not only as one who may need to be physically fed, but as one who seeks nourishment for my soul?

Christian insights

To age wholly will be different for each of us. There are, however, some common threads that Christians may consider as we age. Our incorporation into the life of God is reflected in each human person understood as the image of God. By our baptism we are made whole and by the nourishment of the eucharist (or holy communion) we are sustained; we become what we already are and what we will yet be. What does it mean for Christians to live out this promise well into old age? Here are a few reflections:

- *We are created to be for others, not for ourselves.* Rather than the 'me generation' of contemporary culture, we are called into dialogue, into relationship with one another. For me to age wholly I need you. In the community of the church this is enacted in the warmth of our fellowship and the depth of our pastoral care.

- *We are created unique and diverse.* Ageing for one person will be different from ageing for another person, each one of us equally whole because we are equally loved by God. Of course we will admire those who remain mentally and physically active and productive into old age, but we will not draw unfavourable comparisons with those who age differently.

- *Suffering is part of the human condition.* This is an unpopular view in contemporary society, but not to say that all suffering is inevitable and necessary. It is to say that unavoidable suffering may have an enriching, inherently transcendent value. We have come to believe life should be characterised by the immediacy of sensate pleasure and comfort; anything else is an aberration to be annihilated. In contrast, the Christian gospel would have us embrace life in all its fullness, its joy and its suffering.

- *For a community to age wholly is to ensure every person is encouraged towards healthy ageing.* It is also to ensure that those who become ill and dependent on others receive the necessary assistance and skilled care; and that they continue to be treated as whole persons in spite of their frailty.

- *We are not diminished by frailty or disability.* Personhood is not lost when cognitive powers fail. To speak of a person with dementia as someone 'lost to Alzheimer's disease' is to locate wholeness in cognitive powers alone. While this seriously debilitating disease fractures some relationships, dementia does not make a person less whole. We – who think we are whole – need to seek new ways of relating to the person who is apparently 'lost'. The New Testament has many ways of reminding us that when we draw our own conclusions about who's lost and who's found, our perception may be found wanting.

- *One of the most basic loyalties owed to another is the loyalty of watching, waiting, keeping company, standing by* (McNamara 2001). This commitment is not dependent on words, explanations or right answers, but touch, closeness, one person being alongside another.

- *We are called to bear one another's burdens.* Therefore, if we become frail and dependent upon others it is no cause for shame; it is of the essence of our humanity to care for one another.

- *Human life is finite, moving inexorably toward death.* While death in biblical terms is 'the last enemy', it is not to be perceived as a medical or existential failure. We face death with confidence because God, in the humanity of Jesus Christ, endured human suffering and conquered death. He has already gone before us, with the promise that our life will never be lost, even in death.

- *The quality of our life is not judged in terms of productivity or utility, outward appearance or even the state of our mind.* In God's gracious generosity, our identity does not depend on *who* or what we are in terms of our capacities or incapacities, but *whose* we are in the totality of our being.

It follows from the discussion thus far that the totality of our being is not divorced from the web of relationships in which we find ourselves. Thus, issues of ageing and well-being do not belong to isolated existence or to individual problem-solving in response to the diagnosing of deficits. The issue at stake is the meaning inherent in becoming old. If we see no meaning in ageing beyond decay, dependency and death we will do all in our power to abolish it. If we see ageing as the perpetual striving for perfection, then we will reach the point of despair when perfection is not achieved. If, on the other hand, we recognise the dialectic of ageing, we will see every person as unique and irreplaceable. We will welcome each other in our difference and diversity. Our personal future will not be constrained by cheerful optimism, or by frenetic attempts to keep old age and death at bay; we will see in our finitude not failure to thrive or survive, but a sure and certain sign of freedom, promise and hope, even in death. Karl Rahner, renowned Roman Catholic theologian, confessed this peaceful confidence shortly before his death at the age of 80:

> The real high point of my life is still to come. I mean the abyss of the mystery of God into which one lets oneself fall in complete confidence of being caught up by God's love and mercy forever. (Rahner 1990, p.38)

Holy

When we come to the third 'holy' we dare to enter the realm presumably set apart for particularly holy or spiritual people, hastening to exclude ourselves at every opportunity: 'I'm a nurse, I don't get involved in spiritual issues', or 'I'm not religious, you'll have to speak to your minister about that', or 'I'm a pastoral care worker, not a theologian, I can't answer those deep questions', or worse 'I'm a theologian, not a pastor', or worse still 'I'm only a lay person'. And now dear Liza (with further reference to our 'theme song'), the hole in the bucket is getting bigger and bigger!

To equate holiness with a piety impossible to achieve, to designate as holy those persons who belong to a special category of saintliness, to confuse holiness with human perfection, is to misunderstand the source of all things holy. Alan Lewis acknowledges the protest of those who remain incredulous that Christians lay claim to holiness in spite of our 'perverse ecclesial history of recalcitrance and faithlessness', reminding his readers that being holy does not depend on our accomplishments but on the 'outrageous grace of God' (Lewis 2001, p.370).

God, through the humanity of Jesus Christ and in the power of the Holy Spirit, joins the human community to the triune community, granting us the gift of holiness and wholeness. This gift is also promise, recognising that we will never (in this life) fully realise our calling to be holy. This is not, however, an excuse for inaction. Rather, it is a call to act with and for all persons who are ageing, to share the narrative, helping to shape not only the present chapter but the end of the story.

A primary scriptural reference for the word 'holy' is 'those who are pledged to obedience to God', but since it refers to the whole people of God it also includes those who are ungodly (Bromiley 1985, p.735). We're all in this boat (or leaky bucket) together. What does it mean to care for one another as 'holy' persons? It does not mean that we transport ourselves to some place other than the everyday existential reality of our unique and particular circumstances; nor does it mean a flight from the particular to some generic notion of spirituality. Rather, to care for one another is to attend to *this spirit in this body in this particular place*. There is no Cartesian reductionism at work here, no artificial separation of body, soul and spirit; rather a focus on the whole person as holy person. Could this *particularity* show us the way to a holy trinity for ageing, spirituality and well-being?

The threads of this discussion are now to be gathered into a brief excursus into trinitarian theology.

The Holy Trinity

Theology is not a disembodied pursuit of knowledge and the Trinity is not an inaccessible piece of ancient dogma irrelevant to our daily experience. Trinitarian theology has a direct relationship to the topic under discussion because it is profoundly personal and deeply relational. God in three persons, Father, Son and Holy Spirit, shows us the unique particularity of each person, inextricably bound to the other. In other words, the trinitarian relationships reveal to us the meaning of unity in diversity; that each of us is uniquely irreplaceable and each of us reaches our potential not on our own but through our various relationships.

Trinitarian theology reminds us that we are whole persons only by being in a community of mutuality and interdependence; the foundation of this community is love. In this community our unique individuality is not subsumed; rather our humanity comes to full expression.

Conversation

The Holy Trinity is also about individual address and response: a conversation. Therefore, in belonging to this community we find our identity as those who address one another and respond.

For Robert Jenson the divine persons in mutual converse are characters in God's drama, into which we also are invited (Jenson 1997a, p.75). We enter God's history, and therefore our own, through narrative. Through the drama of God's interaction with the history of Israel, and through God's continued faithfulness to the whole of creation, we are called to participate in this very personal story. 'A person is one whom other persons may address in hope of response' (Jenson 1997a, p.121). There is no sign here of power relationships, nor of problem solving; no presumption that one person has superior knowledge to impart to another. Rather, there is acknowledgement that issues of ageing, spirituality and well-being belong equally to us all.

Loving relationship

In trinitarian personhood there is no hierarchy. The Spirit is not superior to the Son, the Son is not inferior to the Father, nor are the persons of the Trinity interchangeable. The Father is not the Spirit, nor can the Son be replaced by the Father. Each is unique and irreplaceable but each cannot live apart from the others. The driving force of this relationship is love. The Father stoops down in love to envelop the whole creation into a personal relationship; through the humanity of the Son, God experiences our deepest wounds; and through the continued presence of the Spirit we become whole, and holy, persons. The unavoidable corollary is that we then reach out to others and respond to others in love, our humanity enriched by the humanity of others.

The wounded God

When we look to wholeness and holiness from a Christian trinitarian perspective we may see imperfectly, as through a glass darkly, for we are faced with the ultimate mysteries of life and death. When Dennis Potter was dying, that now famous interview with Melvyn Bragg was recorded. Potter's attitude towards death and dying was not of unequivocal certainty or ready-made answers. For him religion was 'the wound, not the bandage', indicating that God is not the filler of gaps (Potter 1994, p.5). The old song asks about the hole in the bucket: 'With what shall I mend it dear Liza, dear Liza?' Potter reminds us powerfully to look at the hole itself; to see life as flawed and imperfect; to see God's presence not in some remote place outside of our experience but in the wound itself. Otherwise, we may see God merely as the bandage, the one who should always come quickly to cover up our wounds. As the wounded one himself, through the nail holes in his flesh, Jesus Christ enters our human frailty, and, through his own broken body on the Cross, suffers with us even in our disease and our doubt and our death. Through his brokenness we are made whole and holy.

Invitation to engagement

To include an excursus into the Holy Trinity in a book on ageing, spirituality and well-being is not to invoke some esoteric, metaphysical concept devoid of existential relevance. It is to understand the human person not as an isolated monad but as living in community, incorporated into a web of relationships. For Jenson, this is to understand our relationships not only as conversation, narrative and drama but as musical harmony as well. Jenson maintains that to be 'harmonised' is to belong to an intricate web of relations 'which is of course increasingly the vision of the sciences, insofar as their practitioners allow themselves to see it' (Jenson 1997b, p.41).

A distinctively Christian view of ageing is not therefore at odds with an increasing acknowledgement in the scientific world that life is relational. The emphasis of this chapter is not intended to impose an artificially 'Christian' perspective onto a broader understanding of the human person; neither is it to suggest that Christians have a monopoly on ageing well. It is, however, to see in trinitarian theology an invitation to engagement. Thus the three persons of the Trinity call us into a community of relationships where our unity in diversity is welcomed. Here, in partnership and dialogue, we find our true selves and hence the vital core of spirituality. 'The Trinity thus appears as a comprehensive model for making sense of human spirituality' (Williams 2000b, p.168).

To repeat the thrice-holy litany is to enter a relationship with God and with each other. And the purpose of this relationship? Not to make us divine or 'holier than thou' but to make us truly human. This is the essence of spirituality, this is the key to ageing well, realised at every age and at every stage of our created existence.

CHAPTER 7

Older People and Institutionalised Religion

Spiritual Questioning in Later Life

Peter G. Coleman

Introduction

This chapter describes a series of related studies carried out on the subject of older people's attitudes to religion and to Christianity in particular – a faith to which virtually all the people we interviewed had been introduced in childhood. It also indicates some of the implications for pastoral care and outreach to this growing sector of the population.

The ideas behind these projects and their execution owe a lot to a number of colleagues in Southampton. Among these I should like to name in particular the first psychology PhD student I supervised, Andrew McCulloch (now Director of the Mental Health Foundation), who identified the importance of studying older people's attitudes to religion as part of research on adjustment to social change. I also gratefully acknowledge the major contributions of my long-term research collaborator Marie Mills, an experienced professional in the field of elderly care and a qualified counsellor as well as researcher, who is currently conducting a study for the Nuffield Foundation on this topic, and of Revd Prebendary Peter Speck, recently retired Chaplaincy Team Leader at Southampton University Hospitals NHS Trust, whose initiatives in providing and evaluating spiritual care have been the stimulus for much of our recent work in this field.

A common theme in all this work has been spiritual questioning in later life. Far from being a time of serenity, old age – at least in our society – can be a time of painful questioning of belief, often in isolation and unsupported by organisations such as churches which might be thought to be natural sources of support.

Ageing, spirituality and religion

The study of ageing and spirituality has been a neglected subject in Britain. The situation is changing now thanks to the efforts of such organisations as the Christian Council on Ageing, MHA Care Group and the Leveson Foundation, the latter specifically addressing the issue of the integration of spiritual perspectives with welfare policy for older people. But within the broader British gerontological community, which in other ways has been so supportive of widening the range of discussion on old age, there has been a reluctance to include the spiritual dimension. Only now do I begin to hear colleagues in the study of ageing agree that the spiritual and religious needs of older people are important subjects which deserve inclusion in consideration of topics such as quality of life.

Why has there been this neglect? A major part of the reason, it has to be said, is to do with the lack of sympathy, even downright hostility, to religious belief on the part of the academic community. This aversion is also found in large parts of the cultural elite in British society, especially among media people and policy makers. The contrast with the USA, where religion is an important part of community life, is striking. Within the UK religion has come to be seen as a minority pursuit, without yet having benefited from the protection afforded to minorities. As one of my first heads of department in Southampton said to me when the university's department of theology was axed, it was important to maintain religious studies within a university – but as part of the archaeology of human belief.

Within recent years, there has been a sea change in attitudes to the social and psychological significance of spiritual belief in Britain and other western European countries. It is important to note that it is 'spirituality' rather than 'religion' that has become the focus of interest, particularly the contribution of spirituality to general health and well-being. However, the concept of spirituality is notoriously difficult to tie down. As a result it is not as readily amenable in the way that, for example, religious practice is to standard forms of scientific enquiry which rely on neat definitions.

It is striking how many of the speakers at the Second International Conference on Ageing, Spirituality and Well-being were concerned about this issue and attempted to provide their own definition. These will be found within the chapters they have written. Although I shall later provide a definition of spirituality which has guided our own research efforts in this field, I do tend to accept the view that 'spirituality' is better viewed as a broad cluster concept, similar to the concept of 'health'. Perhaps the use of the term 'spirituality' should be allowed to range over a wide field, denoting a spectrum of related activity and experience rather than a clearly measurable entity.

The continuing aversion to the study of religion seems to me to be a more significant obstacle to advances in understanding. 'Religion' was not in the title of the conference which underlay this publication. Would it have put people off coming if it had been? I should like to be slightly provocative here and question the growing polarity between spirituality and religion. The former has come to be generally accepted as life enhancing, whereas religion is often regarded as an outmoded and unnecessarily restrictive form of thought, feeling and behaviour. Yet in practice it is hard to divorce the spiritual expressions of most people from their roots in established forms of traditional religious belief and practice.

Perhaps this is expressing my sense of the present zeitgeist too starkly. I know, understand (I think) and admire the work of hospital chaplains who seek to minister to the whole hospital community, not just to the committed Christians and other faith believers among them. To achieve this they often feel that they have to carefully eschew religious language and be prepared – and to communicate this preparedness – to start from where the persons are, and to accompany them wherever their questioning of meaning leads.

But at the same time I think we are in danger of underplaying the value of religion. The Centre for Policy on Ageing report on religion and spirituality in later life (Howse 1999) has raised the social policy implications of the decline of religious allegiance in the population. If many people in the past have relied on religion to provide existential meaning in later life, what will happen – what is already happening – when religion loses its traditional hold? Can spirituality in its newly defined forms take the place of religion? For example, what about the obvious social benefits of religion which are of particular interest to policy makers, such as a sense of community and belonging as well as access to help and services? Membership of well-functioning churches and other religious organisations typically provides these benefits.

The Southampton Ageing Project

When I first came to Southampton in 1977, after spending five years working in a gerontological education and research centre in the Netherlands, I was involved in the planning of a multidisciplinary, longitudinal study of ageing which we have been conducting now for 25 years. We included some questions on religion. They provide some markers in time about older people's religious allegiance. When I finally spoke about our longitudinal data on this subject at the annual conference of the British Psychological Society in Oxford in 2000, it hit the headlines in the newspapers – the first and only time that has happened to me. There was even an editorial in the *Guardian* headed 'Unfaithful unto Death'. The British media are quick to highlight data on religious decline. I was also asked to have a live discussion on the radio with the Anglican Bishop of Southwark. He was understandably apprehensive as to what my approach to the subject might be, that I might be set on demolishing the future of religion.

Table 7.1 sets out the figures on change in reported significance of religion in our Southampton sample over the first ten years of the study. This shows that whereas over two-thirds of the sample regarded religion as an important element in their lives in 1977–8, this number had fallen to less than half in 1988. Assuming that our data are representative of Southampton and that Southampton is broadly representative at least of the south of England, what explanations are there for this striking decline?

One strong possibility is that they reflect the declining respect for authority generally in our culture and society over this period of time – a point I shall come back to – but I think there are also aspects of the decline particular to ageing. For example, a number of our participants referred to their disappointment with their church's response to the death of their spouse. One man, once a very active church member, gave a very explicit account of the distancing he experienced after his first wife died suddenly

	1977–8 to 1988 (n = 101)
Table 7.1 Southampton Ageing Project: change in reported significance of religion 1977–8 to 1988	
Religion continues to mean much	45 (45%)
Religion continues *not* to mean much	27 (27%)
Religion did not mean much, now does	3 (3%)
Religion did mean much, now does *not*	26 (26%)
Total	101 (100%)

four years before the beginning of the study: 'I felt very let down with religion… After the funeral the parson just said "Cheerio, I'm off" and nobody even bothered whether I was all right or not… I've nothing against the church, the teachings of the church…but it doesn't bother me that I don't go to church.' Such observations were the starting point for our most recent study, to which I shall return later.

Questioning of values, meaning and belief in later life

In the literature on the psychosocial tasks of ageing, Erikson's theory of life stages has pride of place (1963). It was the first major attempt to formulate a developmental theory of human life encompassing the whole lifespan from birth to death. The stages are described in dialectic terms as the person faces new challenges to which he or she may respond positively or negatively. Writers on spiritual development also draw heavily on Erikson's concepts (e.g. Fowler 1981; Whitehead and Whitehead 1980). His description of the life stages emphasises both the interrelationship within the successive phases of the single individual life and the necessary reciprocity between generations required for human development to occur. Old people need young people just as young people need old people.

Erikson's discussion of the last task of life – 'integrity vs. despair' – raises at least three fundamental issues about adjustment to the awareness of the ageing process and the closer proximity of death (Coleman 1993). The first is acceptance of the past without bitterness. Acknowledging the limitations on what is possible in one lifetime, the person accepts what has been given, both the pleasant and unpleasant aspects of life, and gives witness to its integrity. This aspect of Erikson's conceptualisation of the developmental task of ageing has received most attention. Reminiscence and life review work are now seen as essential aspects of constructive listening to and counselling older people. The literature on practice in this field continues to expand at an impressive rate (e.g. Webster and Haight 2002).

The second and third tasks, acceptance of one's own death and acceptance of the society that will continue after one's own death, have received much less attention. Being at peace with the idea of the finitude of one's own life and its growing closeness is a natural fruit of acceptance of the life one has lived, but not only this. It also depends on an acceptance of life in general, and in particular of the kind of society that will continue after one's own lifetime. Much of Erikson's theory, especially about the importance of identity formation in adolescence and young adulthood, reflects his concerns about the influence of modernity on human development. This is also reflected in his thinking about the importance of adaptation to social change in later life. The psychological task that Erikson identifies here is not new, but rather a perennial issue in human society. The writer of the book of Ecclesiastes comments: 'Never ask why the old times were better than ours: a fool's question' (Ecclesiastes 7:10).

Nevertheless this tendency to praise the past and deplore the present is likely to be stronger in a fast-changing society such as ours. As a consequence it may be harder to die well in a society that has developed out of the capacity of one's understanding. In earlier research (Coleman and McCulloch 1990) we identified various possible attitudinal reactions to social change: for example, 'moral siege', by which the person retreats from contact with the outside world, often in community with others who share the same values; and the opposite extreme of identification with the changing fashions and habits of the young and unwillingness to 'grow old'. Neither of these responses fits Erikson's concept of 'integrity', which requires rather the ability to be critical and appreciative both of the past and the present, and more importantly to be able to perceive continuity in underlying values guiding life, despite change.

In our studies we identified a common further state of disturbed 'questioning', in which the person is unable to integrate their perception of present and past standards of behaviour and is left in a confused state; for example, unable either to condemn the young for their transgressions or to promote the values by which their own life had been led. This attitude of mind we found to be closely associated with low states of morale. A follow-up of this sample ten years later, which was conducted by Richard Hastings and me, showed no indication that people who had expressed such attitudes had yet resolved their dilemma.

'Questioning' appears to be central to Erikson's concept of 'integrity'. The dialectic inherent in all life's stages requires people to feel the tension in order to develop. Thus the possibility of despair must be real in order to be able to 'tilt the balance' in favour of integrity (Rosel 1988). But tension and struggle are not what we normally expect of older people, who we hope – often for our own peace of mind – to have already overcome life's trials.

This expectation of stability and serenity extends also to the churches that often appear unprepared for the emergence of doubt following the various losses and crises of old age, especially chronic illness, disability and bereavement. We have observed in our own interviews how often the questions about a good God who allows the innocent to suffer appear in older persons' minds as if for the first time.

The most clear cases of loss of faith as a result of severe or prolonged questioning were again related to bereavement (Coleman 1992). Thus one woman, aged 68 years, described how when her husband died of lung cancer some years earlier, shortly after he had retired and they had moved to a retirement area on the south coast of England, she felt that he had not deserved to die and she did not want to go to church any more. She moved back to the area where they had lived before. When no one from the local church came to see if she was all right she questioned even more. Although she felt that she was missing something she could not bring herself to go back to church. Then one day some people called on her from a local Christian group and showed interest in her, inviting her to their meetings. She did not go there for long because she felt she could now go back to the local Anglican church. But she was grateful for the help that she had received from those she described as her 'callers' who had helped her resolve her questioning. She felt the experience had made her faith stronger.

Influence of strength of spiritual belief on bereavement experience

Our contribution to the recent Economic and Social Research Council (ESRC) research programme (1999–2003) examining the quality of later life was to assess the influence of strength of spiritual belief, and the support received for that belief, on the experience of bereavement (Coleman *et al.* 2002). This is the first time that the spiritual dimension has been included in a national programme of research on ageing. In drawing up our proposal we reasoned that loss of spouse in later life, an inevitable crisis that one at least of the couple will experience before their own death, is a circumstance where the presence or absence of spiritual belief was likely to be strongly felt.

For this study we used the definition and measure of strength of spiritual belief that Michael King and Peter Speck had developed for their own studies with patients on hospital wards in London (King, Speck and Thomas 2001). In their measure a spiritual belief is defined as 'a person's belief in a power apart from their own existence...that transcends the present context of reality' (pp.1015–6). The five-item scale has good internal reliability and is useful for providing a simple classification of persons with a strong belief in such a power, with little or no belief, and those with moderate belief. This form of clearly expressed but uncertain belief in a spiritual power capable of operating in their lives appears to be particularly well represented in the older population. In our sample of 28 bereaved spouses, 11 (39%) displayed moderate belief.

We were funded to carry out an intensive study of these individuals over one year, beginning just after the first anniversary and ending just after the second, with an interview halfway between. The three interviews allowed us to deepen progressively our understanding of our participants' beliefs, the factors influencing them and the support they received for their beliefs. All those who indicated a strong level of belief in a spiritual power attended church, prayed regularly and believed in life after death. We administered general measures of health, including mental health, as well as a specific assessment of depressive symptoms, and also scales of personal meaning developed by the Canadian researcher Gary Reker to operationalise Victor Frankl's theoretical model of the relevance of meaning to well-being (Reker and Wong 1988).

Despite the relatively small size of the sample, the results of our study were very striking (see Table 7.2). Depressive symptoms were concentrated among those of moderate to weak belief. A significant number of them also indicated below the norm scores on both personal meaning and existential transcendence. However, it is noteworthy that some people of moderate, weak and no spiritual belief scored high on these scales too, which demonstrates the independence of the measures of personal meaning and spiritual belief. This is the pattern of results we expected. It accords with previous studies, for example, which show that death anxiety is concentrated among those of moderate levels of belief (Kalish and Reynolds 1976), and confirmed our interest in those of moderate to weak belief.

Table 7.2 Spouse Bereavement Project (2000–1): relationship of strength of spiritual belief to depressive symptoms and perceived meaning in life

	Marked depressive symptoms	High levels of personal meaning	Low levels of personal meaning
Strong spiritual beliefs (n = 8)	0	6	0
Moderate spiritual beliefs (n = 11)	6	3	7
Little or no spiritual beliefs (n = 9)	2	3	2
Total	8	12	9

Our case study format allowed us to explore these issues at the level of the individual person and to raise further questions for enquiry. For example, we were surprised by the lack of contact moderate believers had with religious ministers, even when they attended church on a regular basis. One 65-year-old widow said that she went to her local parish church in the hope of cultivating belief. She envied believers their faith. She hoped someone was listening to her prayers, but was more inclined to believe in the operation of a 'cold fate'. As she grew older she felt she believed less and less, and in this thought that she was contrary to the norm for older believers. She was disillusioned by human nature and explicitly stated that she was not at peace with her beliefs.

Another participant, a widower, also 65 years old, said that he liked to sit quietly in church but outside service times. He had an antipathy towards church authority, perhaps reflecting his experience in army service and also with his disciplinarian father. He prayed regularly, feeling he 'owed someone something', and found it helpful in dealing with the loss of his wife. Although religion had come to mean more to him – especially the moral teaching contained in the Bible – he had great difficulty in understanding God as a person or Jesus Christ as God. He said he would like to understand more, but like other moderate believers in our sample he did not seem to be aware of opportunities that he might have to discuss issues of faith.

At present Marie Mills and I are carrying out a study for the Nuffield Foundation to examine, in a much larger sample of older people, their attitudes to their faith and the responses they receive from their churches and other religious organisations to which they may belong. This research has been made possible by an article printed in *Saga* magazine about our ESRC study which highlighted the need to support belief in later life and not to take it for granted. Over 400 people responded to this article and Nuffield agreed to fund a follow-up questionnaire and interview with a proportion of them. The extent of the interest shown in our research and subsequent co-operation with it have been strong evidence for the importance of the subject of faith to older people.

At present we are only just beginning to analyse the data we have collected in this study, but one evident point is the number of queries that our participants have raised in regard to the various propositions of faith contained within the Christian creed: including the virgin birth, the crucifixion, the resurrection, the ascension, the second coming, both the divinity and humanity of Christ, the trinitarian conception of God, the meaning of redemption, and eternal life. People vary considerably in the particular propositions that they have difficulty with, but reading these queries together suggests that it is time to repeat the hard work of formulating Christian doctrine engaged in by the early Church. Many of these older people would themselves like to receive better education in their faith and feel that they have had to rely for too long on the faith that was communicated to them as children.

Conclusion

We appear to live increasingly in a time of personal rather than shared faith – of heterodoxy rather than orthodoxy. Heelas has captured this situation well:

> Rather than authority and legitimacy resting with established orders of knowledge, authority comes to rest with the person... Postmodern religion is very much in the hands of the 'free' subject... People no longer feel obliged to heed the boundaries of the religions of modernity. Instead they are positively encouraged to exercise their 'autonomy' to draw on what has diffused through the culture. (Heelas 1998, pp.4–5)

Clearly there are benefits to greater autonomy in matters of belief, but there are also losses resulting from the dissolution of strong worshipping communities buttressed by shared tenets of faith.

Moreover the issues at stake are much more fundamental than the psychological and social gains and losses (autonomy, individualisation, community and isolation) involved. As the philosopher Charles Taylor has observed in his reflections on William James's classic text *The Varieties of Religious Experience*, the contemporary stress on individual spiritual belief and experience, for which James was one of the first advocates, neglects an important aspect of religious experience:

> The link between the believer and the divine (or whatever), may be essentially mediated by corporate, ecclesial life... What James can't seem to accommodate is the phenomenon of collective religious life, which is not just the result of (individual) religious connections, but which in some way constitutes or *is* that connection. (Taylor 2002, pp.24–5)

Most forms of Judaism, Islam and Christianity – Protestant as well as Catholic – emphasise God's relationship with the community. The contemporary negative view of church authority is in contradiction to this long tradition. Relationships within the religious community are thus of central importance to any consideration of religious or spiritual life. Personal spiritual experience does not of itself give anyone a privileged status.

The isolation of older people – and of people of any age – from religious communities needs to be combated by greater efforts to create opportunities for dialogue, education and, above all, interrelationship. Both spirituality and religion essentially involve finding and drawing on relationship. Seen in this light, spirituality is not at all in conflict with religion, no more than an individual person has to be in conflict with the community to which he or she belongs. The community needs must use its resources to help its members. Thus the religious community has the responsibility to provide answers to questions that arise in the individual mind, but for the questions to be answered they must first be heard. Creating religious communities where people are heard is an essential first step.

CHAPTER 8

The Search for Meaning of Life in Older Age

Leo Missinne

Introduction

Reflections concerning meaning of life are not easy to make and not easy to communicate. What is the meaning of life? What is the meaning of my life, and the life of each and every one of us?

It is certainly not my purpose to deal so much with complicated philosophical notions and distinctions. Let us be as specific as possible concerning this topic. What is the meaning of life in older age? Has older age a meaning? This is a very philosophical question indeed, but a question that has many practical applications.

Today, the crisis of old age appears to be a crisis of meaning. Why am I still alive as a frail older person? As a sick or handicapped older person? What is the point of my life? Why do I have to continue to live when I am no longer accepted in our society? All these questions must sound familiar to people who are in contact with sick older people and concerned with their well-being. To reflect on these questions and to arrive at different possible answers will help older people to live as human beings until the last day of their life.

The question of the meaning of life is, as the Buddha told us, not very exciting. He said: 'One must immerse oneself in the river of life and let the question drift away.' Jean-Paul Sartre wrote: 'All existing things are born for no reason, continue through weakness and die by accident' (Yalom 1980, p.428).

The Russian writer Leo Tolstoy talks about 'Life Arrest' in his book *My Religion*. He said: 'Is there any meaning in my life, which will not be destroyed by my own death, which is awaiting me?' (Yalom 1980, p.419). And why not quote Sigmund Freud, who wrote at the age of 73 in his book *Civilisation and its Discontents*: 'Life, as we find it, is too hard for us. It entails too much pain, too many disappointments and impossible tasks' (Yalom 1980, p.449)?

The French writer Albert Camus said: 'I have seen many people die because life for them was not worth living. From this, I conclude that the question of life's meaning is the most urgent question of all.' There is but only one truly serious problem, and that is judging whether life is or is not worth living (Yalom 1980, p.427).

Meaninglessness

Many psychologists will agree that a lack of meaning in life or meaninglessness is frequently the origin of neurotic or psychotic behaviour. The Swiss psychiatrist Carl Jung felt that the clinical syndrome of meaninglessness was a very common phenomenon in his practice as a psychiatrist. He stated: 'A neurosis must be understood, basically, as a suffering of a soul, which has not discovered its meaning… About a third of my patients are not suffering from any definable neurosis but only from the senselessness and aimlessness of their lives' (Yalom 1980, p.21).

Viktor Frankl states that at least 20 per cent of his patients were suffering from an existential neurosis, which has meaninglessness at its roots (Yalom 1980, p.421). Other psychologists, such as Salvatore Maddi (1967, pp.311–25), Benjamin Wolman (1975, pp.149–59) and Nicholas Hobbs (1962, pp.742–8), all agree that the failure to find meaning in life, the feeling that one has nothing to live for, nothing to struggle for, nothing to hope for, the inability to find any goal or direction in life, is many times the origin of disorganised or abnormal behaviour.

But you do not have to be a psychologist in order to see the meaninglessness in the lives of so many people today. It is manifested in the disease of our time, which is the disease of boredom. So many people find their job boring, their marriage boring, their friends boring, their studies boring and sometimes their vacation boring, and some of us will do some self-destructive things in order to feel we are alive.

Why is boredom the disease of our times? Because we are afraid to have pain, to suffer a little. Even the thought that we could suffer one day makes us afraid. There is a kind of 'pain phobia' in our culture. In one of their songs the duo Simon and Garfunkel suggest that it might be better to be a rock or an island and not feel pain or cry.

We all like to go to paradise here on earth, but we cannot because there are two archangels with burning swords at the gate.

What is meaning in life?

Real life is meeting other people, helping fellow human beings, sharing what we have and what we think by loving and working. Life today in our culture is full of stress and competition. Everybody is trying to be the best and the most important person. Life is becoming a rat race, but remember that if a person wins that race he or she is still a rat. In fact, life is a terminal illness, and if we are willing to accept that then we will live every day of our life with passion but also with joy as it ought to be lived, grateful for every day we receive from God.

The search for a life that matters for us and for our fellow human beings is the most important part of human life, and therefore each human being seems to require meaning, or attempts to find meaning in life, at least at certain moments of his or her life.

Each human being, young as well as old, will ask himself that question at different moments in his life. It is a privilege of a human being to ask himself such a question. What is the meaning of my life here on earth? Before we start to talk about the meaning of life in older age, perhaps I should first ask my readers that question: 'Do you, each and every one of you, know what the meaning of your life is?' What will it be or could it be in your older age?

The question 'What is the meaning of my life?' will become more tragic and more urgent when one is in a period of crisis; when one suffers a loss such as the death of a spouse; or when a person feels that the end of life is near – when we are becoming older. In order to better understand the question and the possible answers to that question, let's first explain in a few words the theory that Viktor Frankl applied to older people, and second discuss the results of some research concerning meaning of life in older age.

Viktor Frankl's theory of the meaning of life

Viktor Frankl was a professor of psychiatry and neurology at the University of Vienna in Austria and a survivor of the German concentration camps. He explained his theory in articles and in books such as *The Doctor and the Soul* (1969), *The Unheard Cry for Meaning* (1978), *Man's Search for Meaning* (1984) and many more. Frankl does not challenge the work of Sigmund Freud, Alfred Adler and Carl Jung, his psychoanalytical predecessors. He understands the importance of Freud's description of sexual drives, of Adler's will to power and of Carl Jung's view of man's aspirations towards integration. But Frankl is convinced that what inspires a person most deeply is the will to meaning, the innate desire to give to one's life as much meaning as is possible.

How can a person find meaning in his life? A person can find meaning in life by believing in values; the kind of values which a person believes will explain his behaviour. There are three different categories of values: creative, experiential and attitudinal. Let's explore each of these values.

Creative values

One can give meaning to life by realising creative values, that is by achieving tasks, by 'doing something'. Some examples of creative values are: writing a book; building a house or cottage; organising a group of volunteers; planning a reunion; painting and studying; or generally doing something which keeps someone busy and is meaningful for that person. The point is that a person has to do, to create something, in order to find meaning.

Experiential values

Another way to discover meaning in life is by realising experiential values, by experiencing the good, the true and the beautiful, or by knowing one single human being in all his or her uniqueness, and to experience one human being as unique signifies to love that person. Love, beauty and truth may keep a person alive by providing a reason for continuing to live. The love of their husband or wife gives many people the most profound meaning. The love for their grandchildren is for many older people a real experiential value which will explain behaviour and give meaning to their life. To live in a beautiful room, a cosy place, where they can enjoy beauty, is another example of an experiential value which will give them meaning, which will keep people alive.

Attitudinal values

A person may, however, be in such great distress that neither creative values nor experiential values can give meaning to life. Such a person can still find meaning in the way he faces his suffering, his sickness. By taking one's suffering upon oneself, a person may realise attitudinal values. The possibility of realising values by the very attitude through which a person faces suffering is perhaps the highest achievement possible to a human being. No one can better exemplify what life is all about than a person who is sick or dying. The best lesson about life and health is given by a sick person. Healthy human beings need to be in contact with sick people in order to appreciate their own health.

Frankl illustrated this attitudinal value theory by a story that is often applicable to older people. He tells how a doctor colleague turned to him because he could not come to terms with the loss of his wife two years previously. His marriage had been a very happy one and he was now terribly depressed. Frankl asked him quite simply, 'Tell me, what would have happened if you had died first and your wife had survived you?' 'That would have been terrible,' he said. 'How my wife would have suffered!' 'Well, you see,' Frankl answered, 'your wife has been spared that, and it was you who spared her, though of course you must now pay by surviving and mourning her.' In that very moment, Frankl declares, his mourning had been given a meaning – the meaning of sacrifice (Frankl 1969, p.xiv).

Another example could be found in a letter of an 11-year-old cancer patient called Jason (who is otherwise unidentified). He wrote:

> I think God made each and every one of us for a different reason. If God gives you a great voice, maybe He wants you to sing. Or else, if God makes you seven feet tall, maybe He wants you to play for the Lakers or the Celtics. When my friend Kim died from cancer, she was only six years old. I asked my mom, 'Why did God make her born at all?' But my mom said: 'Even though she was only six, she changed people's lives.' What that means is that her brother and sister could become scientists, who will help to discover a cure for cancer, because they saw how Kim suffered. And like

me too, I used to wonder why God did pick on me and give me cancer. Maybe it was because He wanted me to become a doctor, who takes care of kids with cancer. So when they say, 'Doctor Jason, I get so scared', or 'You don't know how weird it is to be the only bald kid in our school', then I can say: 'Oh yes, I do. I had cancer myself and look at all my hair now!'

Remember that out of sacrifices came the most beautiful people, not out of happiness. All these different values described – creative, experiential, attitudinal – can also interrelate. Some creative values are at the same time experiential. For example, if a person really loves somebody, he will be doing or creating something for the one he loves.

Finding values

How can a person find values which will give meaning to his life? According to Frankl, values are to be found through *dialogue* – non-directive dialogue. In order to discover the meaning of my life, I need to express myself, to talk about it with someone. We can help older people to find meaning in their life by creating some particular circumstances where they can discover for themselves certain values – values that will help them give their life meaning. These particular circumstances are often just the simple willingness to listen – to have or to make time to listen to an older person. By expressing their thought to someone who is listening, they will be helped to discover some values which can give meaning to their life.

Not only dialogue with others but also *contemplation* and *meditation* about ourselves and our surrounding world will help a person to discover the values which will give meaning to life. This is not a quick process. It sometimes takes a long time before one finds and accepts such values. We have to learn as young people to contemplate and to meditate, in order to be able to do it better in our older age. Relaxation is only the first step to find a way to contemplate and to meditate.

In the rushing and noise that are so characteristic of our culture, people not only need leisure time but also time for contemplation and meditation in a quiet place. Each person should have a 'desert' where he or she can be completely alone and can take refuge from overwork and noise. It takes a lot of courage to be alone with one's thoughts. For those who cannot find solitude in their daily way of life, it would be good if they could have their own 'portable desert', not a portable radio, where they can find solitude amid noisy surroundings, and find the answer to questions concerning the meaning of their life by detecting some creative, experiential or attitudinal values.

Nobody can tell a person what the meaning of his life must be. It is a very personal matter. Each human being has to find the meaning of his life for himself. It is, of course, a challenge. Each person has to make a choice, his own choice, by following his conscience. Therefore, education of conscience is the most important of all forms of education. It is possible that a person can be wrong in his choice and believe in a wrong or not the best value (for example, money, prestige, etc.).

However, as Viktor Frankl said: 'I prefer to live in a world in which a man has the right to make choices, even if they are the wrong choices, rather than in a world in which no choice at all is left to him' (Frankl 1967, p.151). Let me put that another way: it is better to live in a world in which it is possible to have Hitlers on the one hand, but also on the other hand Mother Theresas, a world in which it is possible to have devils and saints, than a world where every human being is just an obedient member of a party or group and has to accept a meaning of life dictated to him by forces he cannot control.

What does research indicate concerning meaning of life in older age?

General approach

Influenced by the ideas of Frankl, James Crumbaugh and Leonard Maholick (1969) published a psychometric instrument designed to measure the meaning or meaninglessness in life. This instrument, the Purpose in Life (PIL) test, is a questionnaire which has in its first section (Part A) 20 items to be graded on a 7-point scale. There are two other sections (Parts B and C) in the test which are geared more to individual therapy. The test is standardised and validated and has been applied to different groups of people. More than 50 PhD dissertations have been written which employ the PIL test as a major measuring tool.

In *Existential Psychotherapy*, Yalom (1980) gives us the following empirical research conclusions after reviewing the results obtained from the

Purpose in Life test together with the Life Regard Index of Battista and Almond (1973). He concludes that for all ages, old as well as young:

1. A lack of sense of meaning in life is associated with psychopathology in a linear sense. That means: the less sense of meaning in life, the greater the severity of psychopathology in the person.

2. A positive sense of meaning in life is associated with:

    - deeply held religious beliefs
    - self-transcendent values (a person likes to be better)
    - membership of groups
    - dedication to some cause
    - adoption of clear life goals.

Yalom (1980, pp.459–60) concludes also that meaning of life must be viewed from a developmental perspective. This means that the types of meaning may change over an individual's life. For example, values that give meaning to life at one time may not be the same values at later life stages. In a certain period of life, a person may have creative values which are giving meaning to his life. Then in another period attitudinal or experiential values may give his life its meaning.

Own research

The Purpose in Life (PIL) test was sent to a sample of people aged 60 and over in the Omaha area (Nebraska, USA). Respondents were asked to indicate their age, sex and living situation. Of the 130 questionnaires distributed, 60 per cent were completed and returned.

The results (which have not been published elsewhere) revealed that only 5 per cent of the people felt that their lives had little meaning; 63 per cent of the subjects indicated that their life had definite purpose and meaning. The remaining 32 per cent fell into the indecisive category. Furthermore, people in the late old age group (73–95) scored significantly higher than those in the younger age group (60–72).

The findings that purpose in life scores were higher for the older age group (73–95) is contrary to what people might expect. However, it may be that persons aged 60 to 72 were approaching retirement or had recently retired, and thus were in a kind of transition period in which alternative values needed to be found, to replace work as a primary source of life and meaning. The 73 to 95-year-olds may have already adjusted to retirement and have developed other ways of finding fulfilment in life. Another possible explanation is that those older adults who have meaningful lives simply live longer than those who have nothing to live for. An interesting note is that no significant difference was found between males and females and their level of meaning in life.

Level of meaning did not seem to differ according to whether the person lived alone, with a spouse, with relatives, or in a home for older people. Perhaps how older people view their own living situation is more important than their living situation per se.

Another finding from this study indicates the values from which older people derive the most meaning in life. These values include:

- family
- spiritual needs
- good health
- helping others
- self-reliance.

But despite their emphasis on the importance of good health, many older people felt that illness and suffering could be a blessing too. Illness and suffering was a positive experience for 30 per cent of the sample, and 25 per cent said it was a neutral experience (you have to make the best of it). This could indicate that many older people derive meaning in life through attitudinal values – that is, by facing their suffering with courage. Their suffering has the meaning of a sacrifice. They see it as the will of God which ultimately will produce good fruits for themselves or their friends.

Creative values do not seem to be quite as important, or at least these values were not mentioned very frequently. In practice, many efforts to help the elderly are concerned with giving them the opportunity to engage in creative activities. However, this may not be the best approach in helping older people to find meaning in their life. Experiential and attitudinal values seem to be more important.

The practical implications of our research suggest that people must learn to develop values other than work-oriented ones before they approach retirement. The capacity to enjoy the beauty of a sunset, to love and be loved, or to derive some good from suffering, should be learned at a younger age and that will help a person to have a more meaningful older age.

Conclusions

1. If young people want to have a meaningful older age, it would be good that they learn to respect and to love older people. If they as youngsters disrespect the older generation and see no meaning of life in older age, they will become another example of the theory of self-fulfilling prophecy. They will hate themselves when they are old and find no meaning and pride in their own older age.

2. Gerontologists have to help older people to live as meaningful a human life as possible. They must also help older persons to have a death as meaningful as possible. Sometimes someone's death may explain better the meaning of that person's life. Moreover, life and death are not only meaningful for that person, but life and death may also become meaningful for others. How many families have been reunited through the sickness or death of a father or a mother?

3. There is something to discover in older age, an aspect of life which cannot be known before it. That is the reason why older age may be a 'time of fulfilment'. It could be the best time of a whole life because one has to write the meaningful conclusion of a life journey, when one can take care of unfinished business towards oneself, towards one's fellow humans and towards God. Maybe the social worker, nurse, or human service provider, if she or he is a person who knows not only the science of gerontology but also the art of gerontology, will be able to help an older person to write that meaningful conclusion.

4. Meaning of life is also closely related to the meaning of suffering. Both are aspects of the same human reality. One aspect adds to the dimension of the other. Without suffering many people will never discover the meaning of their own life.

> Without meaning of life, without values and faith in God, in themselves and in other human beings, a person will never be able to detect meaning in his suffering.

Everything that is of value grows slowly. It always takes time and patience to realise something good and valuable in life. Everything has its own *kairos*.

There is a time to live, there is a time to die, there is a time to suffer, there is a time to enjoy. The meaning of life and also the meaning of suffering have their *kairos*, their specific time. It will be known to us if we are patient with ourselves, patient with others, and patient with God. As Rainer Maria Rilke said:

> Be patient towards all that is unsolved in your heart. Try to love the questions themselves. Do not seek the answers which cannot be given, because you will not be able to live with them. And the point is to live everything. Live the questions now. Perhaps you will then gradually without noticing it live along some distant day into the answers. (Rilke 1963, p.35)

CHAPTER 9

The Dance of Life

Spirituality, Ageing and Human Flourishing

Ursula King

Introductory reflections

I have called my contribution 'The Dance of Life' but it should perhaps be more precisely entitled 'The Dance of Life in the Spirit' as the Spirit animates and energises all life. It will become clear later why I am using the metaphor of dance for the spiritual life rather than the more familiar ones of journey or process. It is really about the energy of life in the universe and in us that is Spirit. My subtitle 'Spirituality, Ageing and Human Flourishing' is meant to capture the dynamic and transformative quality of spirituality as an experience, because I connect spirituality with all of life and all our experiences. It is not that spirituality is something very special and very different from life; no, it is in and through life that we practise and experience spirituality and meet the Spirit. And the dance is also between our spirit, the human spirit, and the divine Spirit, source of the creation and animation of all life in the universe.

To begin with a quotation I came across in the publicity text for a book edited by Polly Young-Eisendrath (2000) in the Routledge catalogue Religion 2001–2002: 'At the outset of the twenty-first century people are faced with a spiritual dilemma, where neither secularism nor religion seem adequate... [A] mature form of spirituality will be the hallmark of future years.' This bold statement featured in the catalogue section on the psychology of religion, and it is perhaps more in literature on psychology, psychotherapy and gerontology or in publications for the caring and nursing professions that spirituality and ageing are being linked and reflected upon rather than in traditional books on religion. This is an important point because people who work in theology and religious studies do not primarily relate spirituality to ageing. They think more often of spirituality in quite general, abstract terms, so that spirituality is not analysed into different dimensions in relation to life as lived. It is interesting to see how different professions have quite a different slant in their approach to spirituality.

A mature spirituality

Integrity, wisdom and transcendence are celebrated as the hallmark of a mature spirituality, as is the making of connections. Such making of connections is like weaving a rich tapestry which creates deeper meaning in our lives. Let us consider how such a mature spirituality can be nurtured and developed throughout the maturing process that each of us undergoes when growing older.

We are living in a *new historical time* where growing older does not simply mean living longer than previous generations, but also living without the prescribed, fixed social roles that were given to the elders of traditional societies. This presents us with an exciting new freedom, a challenging task to shape our lives in new ways by making use of this special time as an opportunity to reflect on our life, to act out its deeper meaning and purpose. We are interested in *spiritual well-being* as an ongoing movement and process towards wholeness. This has been called '*a sense of plenitude*' which relates to an inner sense of fulfilment rather than to need, an experience of acceptance and being content.

Biological and social ageing

The Centre for Policy on Ageing (CPA) published an interesting study on *Religion, Spirituality and Older People* (Howse 1999). This includes the following reflective comment, following the presentation of the empirical data that had been collected:

> It is in the idea of spirituality that we are to find our sense of what old age may contribute to the life of the individual and the welfare of the community... There is convergence between (some) religious and (some) secular views of the significance of old age in the human life course, and

on this basis may be built that shared sense of the meaning of old age…
Many people think that the language of spirituality is ideally suited to this
purpose (though others would prefer to talk about wisdom). What
enables it to play this role is the reference to an aspect of life which is
independent of those capabilities which tend to decline in later life. It
points to a category of powers and strengths which can flourish in spite of
biological ageing and may only reach their full maturity in the context of
biological ageing. (Howse 1999, p.101)

I think this is an important quotation because it includes the word
'flourish' and it mentions biological ageing which has to be distinguished
from social ageing. We are getting older biologically as our chronological
age increases, but that in itself does not mean very much. Chronological
age is quite meaningless when one compares people of different ages.
Social ageing relates to social stereotyping that is applied to us or that we
apply to ourselves and others. What value do we assign to old age? What
wisdom do we see in old people? It has been said that we do not value old
people enough; that in western civilisation youth and the young are valued
above all else, whereas the Chinese civilisation perhaps values old people
the most.

Extrinsic and intrinsic ageing

I went to an excellent retirement lecture recently which emphatically drove
home the point that 'Ageing is good news!'. The lecturer spoke about
intrinsic ageing and extrinsic ageing. He distinguished between ageing in
terms of how our body gets older and in terms of how our sense of self gets
older – how most of ageing is not intrinsic but extrinsic, whereby we
succumb to social pressures and assumptions that affect our own self-
image. I found this a very empowering message, for the process of ageing is
closely related to the question of how you see yourself: as very old and
decrepit, or as strong, still young at heart and positive in your attitudes and
thinking? One's own self-image and attitudes to others as well as oneself
have an important impact on one's process of growing old.

I shall first say a little about why I became interested in this topic, then
explain something about my choice of the expression 'the dance of life' as
well as current understandings of spirituality, explore spirituality in

relation to ageing and human flourishing, and finally return to the dance of life and the Spirit.

Why I am interested in this topic

Teilhard de Chardin

The concern with spirituality and ageing has a great fascination for me for two reasons. First, I have been working on spirituality for more than 20 years, but for a long time in general terms rather than in relation to ageing. My research on the French Jesuit scientist and writer Pierre Teilhard de Chardin, who lived between 1881 and 1955, introduced me to what he called 'the phenomenon of spirituality' (King 1996). He understood this as being central to human development; that is to say for the human species as a whole, but also for each individual. Spirituality is the most interior dimension of ourselves, a phenomenon integral to our very life. Teilhard de Chardin also speaks about the taste for life, the love of life which needs to be animated and sustained throughout our life. I have also worked on spirituality and gender patterns, especially women and spirituality (King 1993), and on spirituality in relation to peace and justice, and in relation to education.

When I did my research on Pierre Teilhard de Chardin in the early 1970s, I especially studied his mysticism and his understanding of eastern religions. For this I went to interview many people who had known him and were still alive then. This involved a very intensive week of interviewing relatives, friends and acquaintances in Paris, who were all septuagenarians and octogenarians. For me this was an extremely formative and memorable experience, for I was still in my early thirties then. I met people who were 40 or 50 years older than me and asked them about their experience of Teilhard de Chardin and their impressions of his work. But I also asked them about their own attitude to life and the future. This was really like an epiphany because people were so different in their views on the present and future, and in their attitudes to life and the world. Here were these people, quite old biologically speaking, who were either still very open and hopeful, or were more closed in on themselves, with much less understanding for the young than I had expected.

I still love talking to older people because one experiences such a very wide range of attitudes and interpretations of life. Just recently, for example, I went to see two women, one of whom was 70 and the other 90. The 90-year-old lives in a retirement home and the 70-year-old lives in her own flat. Now the 70-year-old appeared much older in her attitudes and much less lively than the 90-year-old, which was an interesting contrast. So my first reason for writing about this topic is my work on spirituality in general, which I now see much more developing with special attention to different age groups.

My own experience

My second reason is my own personal involvement in growing older and coming to my official retirement age in my professional career. Besides that, my own mother died in the year 2000, at the age of 93. She lived in her own flat until the end of her life and, although she had experienced a physically and economically hard life, with very little education and considerable deprivation, she enjoyed a very happy and wonderful old age. She was fortunate in retaining good health until the end, but above all she was nourished and sustained by the very close contact with my sister who lived nearby and visited her two or three times a week. My mother shared her experiences and those of our lives – important connections which kept her spirit alert and alive. In fact, when I talked to her on the telephone for the last time, she seemed to have so much energy that I was convinced she would live to the age of 100. But she was dead three days later from a completely unexpected, massive heart attack without any warning. That was the end of her life, which is exactly the way she would have wanted it to end, and this was in fact a marvellous grace.

The dance of life

The cosmic dance

Thomas Merton in *Seeds of Contemplation* speaks of the joy of the cosmic dance of life which is always there: 'Indeed, we are in the midst of it, and it is in the midst of us, for it beats in our very blood, whether we want it to or not' (Merton 1972, p.230). This is the largest setting for 'the dance of life' – our belonging to the vast web of life, the ongoing process of becoming, the immense rhythm of being born and dying integral to the evolutionary history of the cosmos itself. We tend to see this rhythm of life more often rather individualistically, yet our own life can be understood as part of this larger universal pattern. Instead of describing it as a journey or a process, I want to compare it to a dance with changing steps and rhythms which can be linked to spirituality emerging in and through life as lived.

We are all familiar with the idea of the biosphere, an idea only formulated in 1875, describing the layer of life around our planet Earth. Pierre Teilhard de Chardin coined another word to describe the layer of thinking and action, the specifically human layer which flourishes, emerges and grows out of the biosphere, yet also remains within it. He called this the '*noosphere*', from the Greek word *nous*, meaning not just our faculty of reasoning, but mind as an integral and synthesising vision, so that *noosphere* could also be translated as the layer of spirit around the earth. Teilhard de Chardin created this word in the 1920s and used it extensively throughout his books, but it was taken up by others and it is now increasingly used by scientists (Teilhard de Chardin 1999). He emphasised that it was not enough to study scientifically the evolution of life and the biosphere, but that we need to study all the phenomena of this specifically human sphere which covers the entire globe and which includes the experience of spirit, spirituality and mysticism.

The *noosphere* is thus really an immensely active web of connections linked to a layer of knowledge and actions. Indeed, because of this creative vision of the *noosphere*, which can be seen as an early anticipation of the worldwide web, some people have suggested Teilhard de Chardin as the 'patron saint of the internet'. I would add that this web also includes the power of love. For love connects us together through the deepest bonds of friendship and collaboration. It includes mutual help and assistance and can motivate us to act together to transform ourselves and the world around us. That is a very spiritual process, and that is the way Teilhard de Chardin saw it.

Our dance

This larger pattern of development, of the spiritualisation of the whole of the human sphere, is something that I compare to a dance. Very often spirituality is seen as a process or development, or it is likened to a journey which begins in one place and ends in another. Yet the journey is perhaps too individualistic an image, for I can go on a journey alone, I can undertake a pilgrimage alone – of course, I can also go in a group. Now a dance can be done on one's own too, but it is more likely to be with two, three or more people. More importantly, however, is that a dance is linked to music and its changing beats and rhythms. A dance is therefore more unpredictable and more dynamic. Of course at one stage we stop dancing, but while we dance, we also touch each other. We get the sense of life, the sense of things happening, the sense of energy, joy and love that can flow out of this experience of dancing. So I like to speak about the dance of life, which is always interwoven with the dance of the spirit. And spirituality can also be seen as part of the dance of human life.

What is spirituality?

It is important that we look at spirituality from many different perspectives, but it is only relatively recently, maybe in the last 10 to 15 years, that there has been a growing awareness of the impact of the life cycle on the understanding of spirituality. There now exists an *International Journal of Children's Spirituality* (produced by Carfax Publishing of the Taylor and Francis group) which relates to the debates among teachers about the spiritual development of schoolchildren across the entire curriculum. The experience of children belongs to one end of the lifespan whereas the spirituality of ageing belongs to the other end of human life.

Potential for growth

It is important to see the relationship of spirituality with the various stages of life in dynamic terms. From youth to adulthood and maturity the dance of life goes on. Our individual development from birth to death is an unfolding of all the potential that we have, much of which we never fully actualise. It seems to me preferable to speak about spirituality as a potential rather than only as a dimension in human beings, for the latter sounds too linear. Present as a potential capacity in every human being, spirituality needs to be activated and realised, and that also means it has to be taught. Humans have the potential to walk and to talk, and also to dance. But we have to learn how to do all of these. We therefore teach our children to learn to walk, to talk, to dance – to acquire all the immensely subtle and complex aspects of human culture.

But very often we do not teach our children enough about how to really develop spiritual awareness, except if we give them the right kind of religious and spiritual education, which does not happen in large parts of secular society, nor does it always occur in a traditional religious environment. The spiritual potential of each human being has to be awakened, trained and practised, just as we need training to develop the potential to make music, sing and dance, but even then not all of us make good singers. Thus spiritually not everybody is equally well endowed and attuned in life.

Spirituality is difficult to define, but I understand it as *spiritual development, a process of growth* that can still go on even when all other growth has stopped and our physical and mental powers begin to decline. For spirituality is linked not only to our deepest inwardness, our innermost being, but also to our awareness, sensibility and capacity for reflection. Spirituality is both a gift and a task – human will and agency are involved in fostering and nurturing it, and the deepest meaning of human identity is at stake here.

We can expand and deepen the meaning of spirituality by relating specific spiritual advice and practical help to the concrete life situations of particular people, both old and young. Many are the ideas and experiences that can act as searchlights which help us to explore the dynamics of spiritual life in a more focused manner. The experience of ageing is one such focus. We are looking at the other end of life's spectrum, the years of maturity, diminishment and decline when our vital energies slowly disperse.

The deepest core

Evelyn Underhill wrote that the spiritual life is 'the heart of all real religion and therefore of vital concern to ordinary men and women', that it is 'that full and real life for which humanity is made' (Underhill 1993, pp.7f and 33). Here the spiritual is seen as the deepest centre and core, the heart of religion, whereas other approaches focus on shared human experience and its specifically spiritual potential. Such a perspective marks spirituality as wider than the exclusively religious. It has also been suggested that spirituality means to be truly awake, to make a project out of one's life, and to consciously strive for self-integration through self-transcendence.

Religious and secular

What these approaches have in common is the contemporary emphasis on the human subject, on individual experience and psychological development. They ground spirituality *anthropologically* rather than *theologically* or *historically*. This is a new way of looking at spirituality, for traditionally spirituality has always been presented from a particular religious perspective as a special calling linked to a process and goal defined by the beliefs of a particular religion. Yet nowadays we also recognise a secular spirituality arising out of secular experiences. The secular world too can provide us with many resources for nurturing spirituality. However, most people still connect spirituality with some deeper religious orientation.

The world faiths possess a rich spiritual heritage that is being reappropriated with a renewed interest today. For example, many texts of Christian spirituality have been published in the series *Classics of Western Spirituality*, which has appeared since 1978 (published in New York by Paulist Press and in London by SPCK). Source materials on spirituality in different faiths can be found in the series *World Spirituality: An Encyclopedic History of the Religious Quest* (published since 1985 in New York by Crossroad and in London by Routledge). Thus we now have better access than ever before not only to the rich spiritual resources of Christianity, but also to those of Buddhist and Hindu spirituality, Jewish and Islamic spirituality, as well as the spirituality of native peoples and that of numerous new religious movements.

Lived experience

Contemporary understandings of spirituality emphasise the dynamic quality of spirituality as lived experience; an experience linked to our bodies, to nature, to our relationships with others and society. It is an experience which seeks the fullness of life, a life that touches the hem of the spirit in the midst of all our struggles of living, and these struggles too can often resemble the whirls of a dance.

A different way of seeing

From yet another perspective spirituality can be described as a different way of seeing – seeing our own lives, those of others and all life on earth in a different light and from a different perspective. It is the discovery of new insight and wisdom whereby we reshape the inwardness of our lives and reflect on the presence and help of God in the midst of all life, but especially in our own hearts. The growth of spirituality is always connected with an inner awakening, a discovery and transforming of one's understanding and insight. It is being responsive to the dance of the spirit across the struggles, the depths and heights of human life.

This development can happen at any moment and at any age in one's life; there are certainly not only old people who are wise, but also some quite young people who can be very spiritual. However, it is generally acknowledged that it is in the older, mature years of one's life, when many of one's personal struggles have been resolved and responsibilities have been lightened, at a time when one can slow down and physically be forced to do so, that one finds more occasions for reflection, for the in-gathering of life's riches and graces, and also an opportunity for a deeper healing of life's wounds.

Spirituality, the process of ageing and human flourishing

I prefer to speak about the 'process of ageing' rather than of 'old age' as a definite stage which, in any case, occurred at a far younger age in previous generations. Ageing is an ongoing organic experience, for we are all involved in the process of getting older from the moment we are born. The process of ageing is integral to human life and involves both biological and psychological aspects. It occurs on a continuum and its different stages are evaluated differently by different individuals. However, when speaking about the process of ageing here, I mean especially the years after the middle and towards the end of life, the years of retirement after one has reached 60, 70, 80 years or more. People are living longer and getting older all the time, and this will also mean that they will increasingly be longer involved in the active world of work.

Stripping away

Old age has been described as a 'journey into simplicity' (Luke 1997), but also a period which involves a change in our time perspective through becoming more conscious of the time left to live. It is a process of 'stripping away' and making sense of one's life. It has been said that there is no time in the human life cycle where there is greater variability between different individuals than there is in ageing. But this brings with it a responsibility and an exciting task of living life to one's full potential, as well as exploring questions of life's meaning and significance arising from one's inner being.

Flourishing

In this context I find very helpful the term 'flourishing', mentioned in the CPA report quoted earlier (Howse 1999) and also used by several contemporary writers. The philosopher of religion Grace Jantzen, for example, to whom I am greatly indebted, has devoted almost a whole chapter to the topic of human flourishing, which for her is a different way of expressing the Christian notion of salvation (Jantzen 1998, pp.156–70).

The notion of 'flourishing' refers back to the Old Testament, the Hebrew Bible, where it is related to abundance. The prophet Hosea (14:7) says that Israel will 'dwell beneath God's shadow' and will 'flourish as a garden', and Psalm 92:12 declares that the righteous shall flourish like a palm tree. In the natural world and the cultivated garden to flourish means to blossom and to flower.

When we speak of flourishing in the human sphere, Jantzen says: 'It denotes abundance, overflowing with vigour and energy and productiveness, prosperity, success, and good health. The concept of flourishing is a strongly positive concept; one who flourishes is going from strength to strength' (Jantzen 1998, p.160).

This positive idea of flourishing relates well to a spirituality that is holistic; more concerned with the quality of life as a whole rather than only with certain aspects. In order to flourish individually as a person, I have to have good relations with others, and people cannot flourish at times of war, strife and dissent. This notion of flourishing can be linked with the whole web of life and our dependence on the entire ecosystem. It stresses the idea of spirituality as being relational and not something individualistic. We may say that ageing can still be seen as a very positive period where people can experience a period of true flourishing.

Natality

Grace Jantzen's book (1998, p.7) takes up Hannah Ahrendt's concept of *natality* and contrasts it with the customary emphasis on mortality, a perspective where we see ourselves on the way to death (Ahrendt 1958). If the emphasis is laid on the opposite – natality – then we stress instead the possibility of new beginnings, of birth and growth, where life goes on all the time and still has room for positive renewal. This perspective is linked to the view that further growth is always possible. If we look at the process of ageing as a period where one can still be of service to others, where one can still find individual fulfilment and empowerment in different ways, then the concept of natality opens up a very hopeful and encouraging perspective for our thinking.

Empowerment

Another helpful concept is that of empowerment which provides an equally important perspective for dealing with the process of ageing. In growing older, one needs to be empowered still to think and act for oneself. Growing older has sometimes been described as a journey into submissiveness, as a period when one is involved in the process of stripping away whilst making sense of one's life. However, I think that too few people consider what is sometimes called the third period of life as an opportunity for flourishing where ageing is good news.

I am very interested in contemporary research that has been undertaken about people who are growing beyond their eighties and nineties and yet are still learning new things. Considering the physiological and biological level, studies show that even at this age new synaptic connections can still grow in the brain if the brain is sufficiently stimulated, for human brains possess what is called synaptic plasticity. We know that the synapses will not grow sufficiently in a baby if you do not nurture it sufficiently – speaking to the newborn child and stimulating it. That is to say brain matter will not develop if the brain lacks the necessary spiritual and psychological input. Now this is also true with older people. They can still begin to learn new things, and through this experience of learning new synapses will still grow in their brain. So it is important to stimulate the brain, to enhance people's awareness to develop new thinking through new learning processes – a most important principle in caring for older people.

We now know of quite a few older people who have learnt extraordinary things, even at the age of 70 and 80. A wonderful example for me is 'Grandma Moses', the famous American woman painter who lived from 1860 to 1961. After raising numerous children and grandchildren on a farm in upstate New York, she decided to learn to paint at the age of 70 and became a very successful painter for more than 30 years. She always remained a very rural woman, but her life and art convey a wonderful, humble sense of presence, radiating her deep love for nature and life. There are no explicitly religious motives in her painting, but her whole work is suffused with a spiritual quality which I would call the transfiguration of the ordinary. Here you have an extraordinary example of someone who has learnt something new and done something extraordinary after the age of 70. I understand that there are also some musicians who began to write music at this comparatively late stage and there are certainly some successful writers who began writing very late in life.

Living contact

These might be somewhat unusual examples, but there are many, many others of people learning a new craft, taking up a new hobby or foreign travel, or getting involved in different aspects of volunteering or charity work. What is very important is to realise that all the physical and medical care for older people remains insufficient if people do not experience living contact by meeting and speaking with others. This is why senior citizens' clubs are so important, whether organised by religious or secular institutions or on the initiative of some individuals. I heard someone say that if he were ever in charge of a residential home, he would ideally like just to pay people for coming in to speak with the older residents, so that they have conversation partners who keep their interests alive.

People want to be spoken to and spoken with, touched and seen. They want to feel really connected, and this at heart is a deeply spiritual need. I had a very old friend who suddenly collapsed and experienced considerable memory loss in her late eighties. When I visited her, I was amazed and delighted because, quite unexpectedly, she talked with me for an hour and a half. During our conversation her face regained such life and so much spirit, there was so much remembering and so much taking part, that I thought she would live much longer and with a better quality of life if someone talked to her with full attention every day.

More recently I met a man who is well over 90 and still busy writing books, corresponding widely and following life, but reflecting especially on questions of religion, faith and spirituality with an extraordinary involvement and concern. I myself am growing older and am daily learning to reflect more on life's deeper meaning, its spiritual nature and promise.

All these experiences make me more intensely aware to ask: What are the *spiritual needs* of people growing older? What *resources* are available to them for developing greater spiritual strength in times of need? Where are *fresh horizons of hope* when the light of life is waning? What special spiritual needs do we have when living longer and alone? Our alienation consists of a *lack of connections*, and this is perhaps our greatest suffering, especially when growing older.

Responsibility

Spirituality is really about making connections, achieving inner spiritual integration of the many separate parts of our lives. Taking full responsibility for our lives can be seen as the ability to respond to the many experiences we have – and the more this is the case, the more we can create meaningful connections and grow in spirit. I like the definition of Samuel Rayan, an Indian Jesuit theologian, who describes spirituality as 'response-ability' (Fabella, Lee and Suh 1992). Taking responsibility for my life means the ability to respond to different aspects of my life, to different people, to different situations. The more I develop that 'response-ability' by taking more responsibility for my life, the more I can develop my connections and deepen my awareness.

This is a very integral way of looking at spirituality and is also comparable to the dynamic steps of a dance. Moving backwards and forwards as well as upwards, in that sense the dance of spirituality intertwines with the whole dance of life. It is this dynamic movement that people of an older generation can see unfolding in all its richness. Another movement of this dance is not unlike that suggested to the young: exploring the possibilities of life by looking both inwards and outwards across the years of life that meet together in our many experiences and can be integrated through inner efforts.

It is very important not to see older people as dependants but primarily as people in their own right. Of course if people are ill they need to be looked after and cared for, but this needs to be done without disempowering them. Once I visited a 106-year-old woman who was living with her daughter and son-in-law. The daughter, herself 74 years old, used to say that I must not hand pills or a book or whatever to her mother, for she has to take them herself; let her pick up her own things, let her go to the bathroom herself, etc. I was shocked at first that the daughter seemed so unwilling to help and thought this was not very kind until I realised the subtle psychology behind her behaviour. It was based on the wish not to deprive her mother of the power to do things for herself. This is much harder and requires much more patience than helping an old person directly. It is a great spiritual exercise for both people involved, for such empowerment in small things can give great strength and determination, which in turn feed the taste for life and for remaining alive.

Spirituality of the senses

Another insight relating to our interaction with older people concerns what I call the development of a spirituality of the senses: to develop the sense of seeing, of speaking, of listening, of touching; to help people see by learning to be more attentive, to see things more deeply, because that is linked to understanding and to seeing things in a wider perspective. This helps to develop much more integral and holistic relations. So *seeing*, especially inner seeing, is important.

Speaking is also important for all of us: sharing our stories, being able to articulate and verbalise our experiences to ourselves and to others; sharing them, sharing our joys and our sufferings. Speaking is living communication through the word. The word embodies, nourishes and sustains life. 'In the beginning was the Word' teaches St John's Gospel, and Christians believe that the Word is both flesh and spirit – and it is profoundly true that the speaking of the right words can embody strong spiritual nourishment.

Then there is *touching*, so important for establishing human contact, warmth and intimacy. Princess Diana was known for always touching people, not only metaphorically but literally, physically. I was reminded of this when I went to see a French lady, well in her late eighties, recently. She was not particularly ill, but she suffered from great fatigue and a loss of appetite for life. She kept saying, 'Oh, I'm so cold, touch me, touch me, just touch my hands.' She wanted just to be in living touch, to feel the warmth of another pair of hands. To hold her hand, to be in touch, established a living link between us, a quiet communication from body to body, which is more than a gesture for it expresses a spiritual connection of human affinity, closeness and care.

The dance of life – dance of the Spirit

I would like to quote from Maria Harris's book *Dance of the Spirit* (1991), which I have used before (King 1999). Harris's book is actually about women's spirituality where she explains the dynamic development of spirituality through the moving steps of a dance, which is what originally inspired me to speak of 'the dance of life'. The book includes practical exercises of centring, awakening, remembering, discovering, celebrating and engaging spiritual insights through the rhythms of life. Harris also uses an inclusive understanding of spirituality related to all of life when she writes:

> Initially spirituality is seeing. This means not just looking, but *seeing* what is actually there, seeing into and entering the deep places and centers of things...our spirituality begins with our cultivating the inner eye that sees everything as capable of being...saturated with God. (Harris 1991, p.65)

Receptivity

Harris also distinguishes between different forms of spirituality that are contemplative, actively engaged, resisting or simply receptive:

> *Receptivity* is an integral part of life, but marks especially those who are bedridden, or palsied, or mentally unable. They are [those] who are ill or old, or in some way *forced* to be waiters and watchers, no longer able, if they ever were, to be completely involved in a physical, questioning, resisting, or empowering spirituality – although their receptivity may itself be a form of each of these. These are the women [and men] who experience life as something to be received in totality and are almost

completely dependent on the care of others. They teach the rest of us much about a side of life that belongs in each of us but is too often ignored: a side of spirituality that sometimes arrives quickly, sometimes accidentally, yet eventually claim us if we live long enough.

At the beginning of life we are full of *physical* energy, but we are also in some sense almost totally *receptive* – waiting for life to come and meet us. At the end of our lives we are forced to be *receptive*, especially as we befriend death, but this is often totally determined by our *physical* circumstances. And in the midst of, as well as in between both physical and receptive life, we all have periods of *questioning*, *resisting*, and *empowering*. (Harris 1991, p.73)

I think this passage expresses a lot of wisdom.

Religious practice

The thought-provoking CPA report (Howse 1999) also comments on the differences in religious practice among older and younger people. Only a minority of older people participate in organised religion, but religion still plays an important role in the lives of a large minority. Yet for many the ageing process itself contributes to a deepening of religious concerns. It is therefore particularly important to develop a general awareness of the spiritual dimension in carers, especially in those involved with the caring for older people. The language of spirituality has become a kind of lingua franca between different religious traditions and refers to 'the cultivation of attitudes of mind and practices that are intended to effect the mental reorientation of human desire and which derive their value from something more than their mere contribution to human well-being' (Howse 1999, p.83).

An oasis for the soul

To use another image, developing spirituality can also be described as creating an 'oasis for the soul'. This links the nurturing of spirituality to a sense of place rather than the activity of dancing by grounding ourselves in a particular 'spirit spot', both in our actual environment and within ourselves by cultivating attentiveness and new ways of seeing. This can create a sense of wonder and spiritual joy, which deeply refreshes our spirit. We can thus truly 'recreate' ourselves.

For many people this happens through particular forms of recreation, often through the experience of the natural world or through different forms of art which draw us out of ourselves into another dimension. These experiences can be widely cultivated in old age, whether through the joy of a garden, the wilderness of the mountains and the sea, the experience of walking, the stillness of the night or the pure light of the new dawn. There is the enjoyment of music, of paintings and sculpture, or of dancing, of celebrating, of experiencing generous hospitality and, perhaps most of all, in being nourished through our relationships with family and friends.

Conclusion

The time of ageing into maturity is thus a time of great opportunity – truly a time of grace where we can work on spiritually deepening our lives. The expression 'growing older' is a very wise one, for we are still growing, but growing in a different way from when we were young. Now, perhaps more than ever before, we have the opportunity for contemplation and meditation, for nurturing wisdom and fostering our spiritual development. Growing older involves adaptation and transformation. It can be an occasion for celebration, but it may also be an experience of separation and isolation. Old age has sometimes been likened to a kind of 'natural monastery' in which earlier roles, attachments and pleasures are being stripped away but such 'cutting off' and shedding of attachments does not have to mean loneliness or disengagement. On the contrary, new insights and experiences can lead to fresh creativity and new energy.

I hope I have shown that ageing can be a positive experience and that spiritual development can still occur at a time when physical and mental powers decline. If we have faith we can discern the hidden dance of the Spirit across the landscape of our lives and feel the helping hand of God in our hearts. If traditional religious meanings remain closed to us we can still see ourselves as participants in the great universal dance of life, described in so much fascinating detail by contemporary scientists such as the biologist Ursula Goodenough (1998) or depicted in television series such as *The*

Blue Planet. The dance has a rhythm and pattern not of our own making or choosing, yet each of us contributes some beats and patterns of their own. Growing older can be a great season for human flourishing, especially when we remain open to the animating, dancing Spirit within and around us.

CHAPTER 10

Magic Mirrors

What People with Dementia Show Us about Ourselves

John Killick

I intend to approach the subject of spirituality in relation to people with dementia gradually, first by outlining briefly historical and current attitudes towards people with the condition and their capacities, then by examining a specific area in which spiritual approaches are currently being explored, finally confronting our subject directly. I have therefore divided the text into three sections:

- defining our approach to dementia
- 'holding a rainbow in our hands'
- seeking the spiritual in dementia.

Defining our approach to dementia

Our starting point is what might be called the traditional view of dementia. It presents itself in the form of an authoritative definition of the condition:

As a result of a degenerative process in the brain, nerve cells become gradually incapable of communicating with one another. The disintegration of the brain tissue leads to a breaking of the communication lines which anchor a person in his own time and environment. His mind goes adrift. Communication with other people and even his own body becomes disturbed. There is total dislocation. The patient slowly but inevitably regresses to the functional level of an ailing, helpless newborn baby. (Souren and Franssen 1994, p.14)

This account is very confident in tone: it does not admit of another viewpoint. Indeed in its use of words like 'total' and 'inevitably' it rules out the possibility even of any gradation of opinion. It presents the 'medical model' in essence, a portrait of radical disruption of the normal resulting in a series of losses of function. In this, it has to be said, it conforms to the perceived experience of many carers who, quite understandably, find it impossible to come to terms with the changes in their loved ones and talk of those they knew as having 'gone away'.

In 1990 Jonathan Miller, president of what was then called the Alzheimer's Disease Society (now the Alzheimer's Society), articulated the approach to someone with the condition as: 'There is this grotesque thing in the corner…an uncollected corpse that the undertaker cruelly forgot to take away' (Miller 1990). Even in 2002 Alzheimer Scotland/Action on Dementia could mount its most costly campaign to date with the byline 'Are You Losing the Person You Knew?' (*Dementia in Scotland Newsletter* 2002), with the words growing fainter as the question progressed. This was a clever fund-raising ploy, if a dubious ethical stance (Bender 2002).

For many years pessimism prevailed in the world of dementia care. It isn't very difficult to instil fatalism into people who are looking after others with a condition so shrouded in mystery: we still don't know what causes dementia or how to cure it. Then in the 1990s along came a psychologist at the University of Bradford to challenge the prevailing culture of nihilism. Professor Tom Kitwood proposed the simple but revolutionary formula: instead of 'person with *dementia*' he put '*person* with dementia' (Kitwood 1997, p.7). This change of emphasis opened up a new perspective on the subject. Kitwood did not stop there. He carried through the implications of his sea change by floating the concept of a 'malignant social psychology' (Kitwood 1997, pp.46–7), whereby in a host of ways the person with dementia was put down, even persecuted, for what had happened to him/her by individuals, groups and society as a whole, through ignorance, fear and impatience.

For many people living or working with people with dementia this has been like a door opening, offering new vistas, bringing hope where otherwise there had only been despair. For if by the way we treat people with the condition we can make things worse for them, conversely if we can improve our communication and empathic skills we can also make things better for them. This has led to the development of a whole raft of therapeutic options, as yet still largely untested, but many offering promising leads.

The emphasis that Kitwood put on the person made it necessary for him to attempt a definition of the concept of 'personhood', one which has become very influential in dementia care: '…a standing or status which is bestowed on one human being, by others, in the context of relationship and social being. It implies recognition, respect and trust' (Kitwood 1997, p.8).

The idea that we treat people with dementia as people rather than afflicted objects was a very necessary corrective, but it is now the case that there are people who wish to take this further and posit the view that the condition may confer certain special qualities upon them which were latent or at least less developed prior to the onset. This is an idea which will be explored in the second and third parts of this chapter.

But before embarking on this there is a further argument for equality of personhood to be made, and this is best exemplified in the writings of the American ethicist Stephen Post:

> We live in a culture that is the child of rationalism and capitalism, so clarity of mind and economic productivity determines the value of a human life… Rather than allowing declining mental capacities to divide humanity into those who are worthy or unworthy of full moral attention it is better to develop an ethics based on the essential unity of human beings and on an assertion of equality despite unlikeness of mind. (Post 1994, p.3)

Here Post is arguing for a morality based on what people with dementia have in common with the rest of us rather than what divides them from us. He correctly identifies a major drawback to this in what he terms our 'hyper-cognitive culture', which values logic and intellectual capacity above such qualities as intuition, creativity, feeling and spirituality. By stressing the equal importance of the latter cluster of qualities we are going against the tide of western civilisation. To stand up for them in society generally is difficult enough, but to promote them in the context of dementia demands obstinacy of a high order.

It also requires courage. Maintaining an unpopular stance against the obduracy of the majority is one thing, but the sheer practical difficulties of holding to the philosophy is another. The concentrated effort, over long periods of time on a one-to-one basis with individuals who are themselves struggling to establish their personhood against what must at times seem overwhelming odds, is a challenge. It is not surprising that some suffer burn-out (Killick 1999, pp.22–4).

Yet once the question 'Can we risk person-centred communication?' is posed, do we really have any option but to engage with the issues? Faith Gibson, Emeritus Professor of Social Work at the University of Ulster, gives her answer:

> We must employ whatever power we have in the world of dementia care for this purpose. We must use our present knowledge, our skills and feelings, to communicate. We are morally obliged to continue working in extending our limited understanding, developing our embryonic skills, and taming our deep anxieties. (Gibson 1999, p.24)

'Holding a rainbow in our hands'

Accompanying a close friend on his journey into dementia, Beth Shirley Brough wrote:

> My heart was rent by the gobbledygook, the rhythmic running together of sounds, but the mumbo-jumbo served a purpose. I wondered if it provided a comforting chant-like state from which other words and phrases could arise. Was it a minimalist message on the tender interface of the conscious and the unconscious? (Brough 1998, pp.52–3)

The borderline between speech and music is easily blurred. Many of those close to people with dementia attest to the power of music to unlock language as well as provide stimulation and solace and, in those for whom the verbal is fraught with difficulties, movement, gesture and dance are alternative methods of expression which can be employed.

Responding to Music is the title of a video and book (Mullan and Killick 2001), one of a growing catalogue of materials being produced at Dementia Services Development Centre at the University of Stirling to ease people into the arts and encourage them to try out new approaches. One of the many striking interactions described is that between Bob, a day centre attender, and Maria, the musician. Maria has just played Bob a piece of Bach on the keyboard:

BOB: You touch the very, the little strings in the centre of my heart. What do you think of that now?

MARIA: I touch the strings in the centre of your heart? Is that how you feel when you listen to music?

BOB: Oh yes, oh yes I do, yes. It's something you can't explain. That's the way it is. There's something in you, like, I suppose mental as well naturally, and I don't know, you can't explain it, that's the way it is.

Of course, music is only one of the art forms available for our use in communicating with people with dementia, and we recognise this in our project: photography, video, painting, stained glass window design and drama have all featured so far. We have taken much inspiration from California, where a collaboration between a care worker and an artist has resulted in paintings of high quality from people, many of whom have never taken up a brush before. This has resulted in a book and an annual calendar. Selly Jenny and Marilyn Oropeza (1993) comment:

> As we stand before their paintings they call out to us in a way we cannot ignore. They tell us their stories in a language we all understand, transmitting feelings and emotions trapped inside. Slipping beyond the language of words, their paintings show us glimpses of who they were and who they still are. (Jenny and Oropeza 1993, book cover)

The quotation helpfully links expressiveness to the continuing existence of personhood.

There is some evidence that some people with dementia develop exceptional talents in specific art forms after the onset of the condition (Miller 2000). There is much anecdotal evidence that a larger number of people post-dementia find themselves in possession of a modest talent in one or more media. This is something which, given the right investment in staffing and training, could bear fruit more widely than at present.

Why should people with dementia be so open to the opportunities which the arts present for self-expression and creativity? Faith Gibson gives us a lead here:

> Dementia strips people down to the essence of their being and frees them
> to be in more direct touch with their emotions. They communicate with
> greater authenticity than our customary conventional reliance on
> controlled emotional expression. (Gibson 1998, pp.6–7)

My own theory is that dementia attacks intellectual capacity and semantic
memory but leaves the feelings and those memories linked to strong
emotion largely untouched. It may be that, because of the losses in some
areas, a person tends to put greater emphasis on other areas to compensate.
This would explain why the affective component of the person often
seems so strongly developed. There is also the characteristic of
disinhibition which in some individuals seems very pronounced. This may
remove barriers to artistic expression which otherwise had prevented
abilities from being recognised.

One day a man in a lounge of a dementia unit leaned across to me and
asked if I had my notebook with me. He proceeded to dictate the following poem:

> In the skies up high
> with the clouds below you –
> that's where I'd like to be.
>
> With the birds,
> the little sparrows,
> but I'll remain a man.
>
> It's an attraction,
> it's the spaces
> that we can't reach.
>
> I was up there one day
> and got the sensation
> I didn't want to come down.
>
> I'd rather be
> a creature of the air
> than of the earth.

(Killick and Cordonnier 2001)

I asked him if the poem should have a title. 'Of course: "The Blue Far Yonder",' he replied. On reflection I saw how appropriate it was. Blue for artists and writers has traditionally been the colour of the imagination, and this certainly appears to be a poem about vision. The third verse seems the key in this regard. The sky is also traditionally the realm where spirits have flown freely. The sense of exploration is a common characteristic of people with dementia, as if they are experiencing the world afresh, its sounds, shapes, colours and scents.

Claire Craig is an occupational therapist from the north of England who has written extensively of creativity in dementia. One day she had just completed an art activity with a woman who turned to Claire and said: 'We have been on a wonderful journey, you and I. What fun we have had, laughing and singing. Holding a rainbow in our hands' (Craig 2001, p.38).

The rainbow seems a particularly apposite metaphor for the experience of sharing with people with dementia. It has its dark side in the rainclouds, and its bright one in the sunshine. The coming together of the two results in something that is both beautiful and mysterious. Yet it is evanescent. Moments of clarity, of wonder, occur with people with dementia, but often they do not last. They are not, however, to be valued any less for not possessing duration. On the contrary, because of their rarity and intensity they are especially to be treasured.

Seeking the spiritual in dementia

I take my definition of the spiritual from Alison Froggatt and Laraine Moffitt:

> In this context we mean the search for that which gives zest, energy, meaning and identity to a person's life, in relation to other people, and to the wider world. Spirituality can be experienced in feelings of awe or wonder, those moments of life which take you beyond the mundane into a sacred place. (Froggatt and Moffitt 1997, p.225)

It is interesting to note that the authors link spirituality with the notion of personhood, and identify emotion as an essential element of the concept. We cannot, of course, through observation be sure that a person with dementia who has lost speech is on an internal journey, or whether, as some would maintain, they have closed down to new experience and forgotten the possibilities explored in the past. But it has been my experience that sitting with someone in the silence or holding their hand or submitting oneself to the prolonged scrutiny of their gaze has proved memorable and fulfilling, taking one out of the context of the ordinary and into a new realm of being. Others who have attained a similar communion confirm that a qualitative leap can be involved here.

One man with dementia attempted to express his aspirations in the following poem which he entitled 'Glimpses':

> to see what is beautiful
> to hear what is beautiful
> they don't know what is beautiful
>
> all these young people
> good men, nice boys, fine chaps
> they are too busy to see
>
> it'll be a good bit longer
> before you see
> what you want to see
>
> but they don't want to see
> what in some queer way
> they are anxious to see
>
> we see it very rarely
> but the difference is
> we are trying to see!

Whilst we may not fully understand the meaning of this poem it certainly communicates a sense of exploration, even yearning. There is no resting on the laurels here, rather an attempt to reach out towards the ineffable.

It is the realm of relationship which, paradoxically, provides some of the most substantial examples of developing spirituality. I say paradoxically because this is precisely the area where so many carers speak of the destruction of pre-existing rapport. But a sense of openness to sharing is vital for such interactions to burgeon and this is where so many carers find it impossible to surmount the barrier of habits built up over most of a lifetime. Where breakthroughs have occurred there are memorable examples of relatives reporting their impressions. Anthea McKinlay is one:

Seventeen months before she died my mother told us that she felt her 'top layer' had been 'stripped'. I am her only child. After a lifetime of barriers and difference between us, we found one another. My mother used a new language to describe her experience. I was learning new ways of being and listening and to be unattached to assumptions. (McKinlay 1998)

Kim Zabbia is another. She is an artist and has painted her responses to her mother's dementia as part of a thesis. Here she is discussing the process with her supervisor, who speaks first:

'May I suggest that you refer to your relationship with your mother as a parallel journey, instead of a single journey?'

'I can't call it a parallel journey. This may sound spooky but it's like Mom and I are one person. It's difficult to explain. It's just that we are so much together in this adventure, this voyage, that we seem almost to be one.'

'That's great, then,' he said sincerely. 'You've apparently landed onto something spiritual and unique.' (Zabbia 1996, pp.171–2)

Perhaps the most remarkable statement of the gifts people with dementia can bring us in the spiritual realm comes from Debbie Everett, a hospital chaplain in Canada:

People with dementia are magic mirrors where I have seen my human condition, and have repudiated the commonly held societal values of power and prestige that are unreal and shallow… Because people with dementia have their egos stripped from them, their unconscious comes very close to the surface. They, in turn, show us the masks behind which we hide our authentic personhood from the world. (Everett 1996, p.167)

In its reference to 'societal values' this seems to chime with the ideas around the 'hyper-cognitive' expressed by Post (1994). But Everett goes further than any other commentator in identifying a challenge thrown down to us by people with the condition: to be as unequivocal in the manner in which we present ourselves as many people with dementia seem to be. It can be highly disconcerting to feel oneself being tested out so directly, but then people with dementia need to know whether we are to be trusted. Many of us, alas, may judge that we have been found wanting.

But the rewards are there in new levels of intimacy and understanding. One woman said to me: 'I bet you've never been so near nature before!' It is a supreme irony that those whose personhood we have had the temerity to question may be the very persons to teach us to see our own personhood in a fresh light and to lead us to re-evaluate human possibility.

CHAPTER 11

Hearing the Story

Spiritual Challenges for the Ageing in an Acute Mental Health Unit

Deborah Dunn

Introduction

This chapter focuses on providing a person-centred environment in which the individual story of a person with dementia may be heard; where they feel listened to and valued. The content describes the strategies developed in response to the desire to meet the spiritual needs of persons with dementia in an acute psycho-geriatric unit, and presents some of the positive outcomes which emerged when responding to the spiritual dimensions of holistic care through participation in group activities; an example being strengthening communication and self-expression through opportunities for telling their own story.

The challenge

Whatever a person's age, each is on a journey. The onset of illness, be it physical or mental, does not end the journey, which in fact continues throughout the duration of the illness and possibly involves a faith journey as well.

Sometimes in later years of life the journey can be filled with obstacles. One example of this is dementia, an illness that often has a devastating effect on individuals, their families and friends. Altered and challenging behaviour patterns create barriers to communication, which is a basic human need. It is therefore important to develop methods of communication that are appropriate to such individuals' diminished abilities, enabling person-centred care which meets their physical, emotional and spiritual needs.

The challenge? To give people with dementia back their voice, to once again enable them to be heard, especially in regard to their spirituality: that which is at the core of our very being, whether we acknowledge it or not. In *Winter Grace: Spirituality and Aging*, Kathleen Fischer writes:

> Spirituality means not just one compartment of life, but the deepest dimension of all life. The spiritual is the ultimate ground of all our questions, hopes, fears, and loves... It concerns our struggles with loss; questions of self-worth and fear of reaching out to make new friendships. (Fischer 1998, p.13)

Spiritual care, in its fullest sense, means concern for the whole person – not just one aspect of the person – and what is meaningful in their life.

As the chaplain in an acute mental health unit, working with people in the acute psycho-geriatric ward, this was the challenge confronting me on the seniors' ward. How do I meet the spiritual needs of people with dementia when they have difficulty expressing basic daily needs, let alone their spiritual needs?'

The difficulty, I found, was one of getting to know the issues for each individual, of being able to connect with them at a meaningful level which allowed me to identify their sense – or lack – of purpose, meaning and hope in their life at this stage of their journey. Because of this difficulty it was apparent that often their spiritual needs, since they weren't known, were not being met. This is especially so in an environment where the medical model, a model that views the person from an exclusively biological perspective, governs practice.

During the Centre for Ageing and Pastoral Studies conference in Canberra in September 2001 an important question was put before the delegates: Does being absent in mind mean being absent in spirit? It has been found that as cognition fades, spirituality can flourish as a source of identity. Working solely within the medical model silences the voice of people with dementia (Cairns 2001).

When caring for people with dementia, or any mental illness, it is important to look behind and beyond the illness or the symptoms – listening to the story so that the carer(s) may reach a fuller understanding of who this person is and perhaps identify any specific need(s) which may be addressed.

Tools for caring

One tool used when caring for the ageing is *narrative gerontology*; that is, using life story in terms of how we work with people in order to gain a better understanding of their current situation or behaviour. This is also useful in gaining insight into where the person perceives himself to be, how they 'fit' and, most importantly, what gives or gave them meaning in life.

Another method that gave insight into how communication and understanding could be improved was the use of *validation therapy*. Simply validation therapy is listening with empathy. Validation provides a practical method for communicating with the aged person, accepting them where they are. This means that unexpressed feelings are not explored, nor are expressed feelings analysed. They are just accepted as being true for that person at that moment. Validation therapy sees all people as being unique and to be treated as individuals. All people are valuable and to be valued, no matter how disorientated they are. Empathy builds trust, reduces anxiety and restores dignity. By travelling back with a person the caregiver can begin to understand their underlying life themes. The outcomes of this type of group work with people suffering from dementia have been encouraging (Bleathman and Morton 1991).

As chaplain, my experience in facilitating group work, incorporating art and discussion, highlighted the usefulness of *groups* as a forum which enabled people to share their experiences and issues in an environment that was not threatening and did not involve the use of numerous questions, but allowed them the opportunity to talk about those issues that were important for them.

'Hearing the Story'

It was with this challenge and these concepts in mind that 'Hearing the Story' was conceived and developed.

The *format* of this group consists of the chaplain as facilitator, a staff member (nursing or occupational therapist) as co-facilitator, and a maximum of five or six people as group members (of whom at least half have a diagnosis of dementia). The group per session average is around four people as group members.

It is a *weekly* group of *one-hour* duration, this being dependent on the number of participants and the amount of sharing that occurs, which will vary from group to group depending on the level of acuity.

The tools or resources offered as a starting point and as a means of facilitating communication are *drawing materials* (such as a circle of paper and marker pens) and *pictures*, which are used on alternate sessions.

Drawings

When using the drawing materials, group members (including the facilitator and co-facilitator) are asked to draw a picture based on the question: What gives you joy in your life? When everyone has completed their drawing in the time allocated (usually ten minutes), each in turn is encouraged to share their drawing and thus their story with other members of the group.

When using this method the outcomes have been varied and illuminating. The drawings consist of images that are issues or concerns for the person, such as figures representing family, or pictures of activities the person used to be involved in that were significant in their lives – for example, gardening or their work as a fisherman.

They may be abstract drawings of how they see themselves at that moment. One such drawing was of a green cage with a pink splotch, which during the sharing was articulated by 'Bill' (67 years old) as being the cage in which he felt trapped, giving the staff member and myself some insight into Bill's sense of loss of control and its impact upon him. This afforded me the opportunity of setting aside time to address with Bill some of the fears and concerns he had. Another drawing was full of those things that had filled 'Clare's' (78 years old) life, indicating to the facilitators what had been important and significant to Clare: her house, garden, being able to cook for herself, sewing, her independence – that she was ultimately losing due to the dementia.

The experience of using drawings as tools for facilitating communication has proved to be a useful one. In one particular group session 'Jack' did not hesitate in completing his drawing. In it he depicted the way to his house and his wife. In his sharing Jack told us that it was a 'new home' and that he hadn't yet been there, but his wife 'May' lives there, whom he said he was missing and had not seen for a month. This proved to be a fairly accurate account of his situation as his wife and family were at that time having great difficulty coping with the changes occurring in Jack due to his increasing dementia and need for extra care and support. The most touching part of Jack's story was when he shared with us that he 'missed being cuddled'. This reminded us of a basic human need to be touched, to be loved.

Pictures

The other tool or resource utilised is pictures. These are cut out of magazines depicting as wide a range as possible of images that may connect with everyday life: pictures such as families of different generations, in different settings and configurations; pictures of activities that are commonly undertaken such as walking, tool sheds, picnics, houses, food, dealing with pets and other animals.

These are spread out on a table and each group member is asked to select two or three pictures that they like. Then each in turn shares why they selected that particular picture and its significance or meaning for them.

Outcomes

The outcomes that have emerged from these groups are encouraging and hopeful.

Family

Insights into family relationships (or lack of them) are raised numerous times in groups, highlighting the need for family connections and support in later life, which gives many of the people in our care, especially women, their sense of purpose. It is what they see as giving their life meaning.

Grief

Another major issue that comes out during these groups is that of grief. On a number of occasions we (the staff member and myself) had not recognised the intensity of grief that person was experiencing. The nature of the group, because it is non-threatening, has enabled each of these people to speak of their grief. On a number of occasions this conversation has continued beyond the group meeting, at the instigation of the person concerned.

It is our experience that a majority of group members have been willing to share such feelings with each other, some being able to share at a deeper level, offering insight into their issues and the grief and pain surrounding them.

Mutual support

We have noted that when common issues or experiences are shared (rather than just speaking and listening to others) then there is support offered to each other. There is 'conversation' generated amongst group members, moving the group to another level of communication – one that is deeper, more meaningful, allowing real interaction amongst the members. On one such occasion the conversation evolved around the sharing of the loss of independence and what it meant to each person. Out of this conversation there came an increased sense of support and camaraderie between the three members involved.

Growing confidence

On another occasion a group member, 'Peter', shared with us that 'I'm losing my confidence'. After this Peter was encouraged by us, as facilitators, to participate in the group as best he could. This was done by allowing him time to express himself, to finish what he wanted to say without someone (especially staff) jumping in and finishing it for him, and by being supportive and understanding. At the conclusion of the group Peter thanked the facilitators and shook staff member's hands very firmly, showing us the deep-felt appreciation of his experience in the group session. To my pleasant surprise Peter stopped me the next day and told how much he had enjoyed the previous day's group – a need met.

Coping with fear

On another occasion, 'Margaret', a group member who was strongly focused on self, participated in the group, sharing deeply with us what she felt and where she believed her life to be. Margaret was full of fear at the changes occurring, feeling loss of independence, isolation and lack of hope for the years ahead. The nursing staff had found Margaret to be a particularly difficult person to work with and there was a lot of tension. During the debriefing following the session the staff member shared with me that she had been unaware of issues surrounding Margaret's treatment having used a 'medical model' of approach, which did not include hearing parts of Margaret's story; parts that until then had been previously unheard.

Staff benefits

What hearing Margaret's story did was to change significantly the understanding and thus the attitude of the staff member (who had been the primary carer) towards her, resulting in a reduction in tensions between them. That staff member was beginning to see and understand 'the person' behind the illness.

Margaret also experienced a change in attitude towards her primary nurse, evinced in an exchange between them when Margaret expressed concern for the nurse's well-being after an incident (an assault) with another patient. When relating this exchange the nurse expressed surprise at the care she had received from Margaret. It appears that the change in perspective and attitude by the staff member facilitated the change in their relationship.

One of the most significant outcomes of these groups is the change in attitude occurring among those staff members who have been co-facilitators towards the people under their care. There have been many 'Wow, I didn't know that' moments which highlight the importance of engaging with people with dementia (or any mental illness) in a manner which is conducive to better communication, while at the same time enabling their individual stories to be heard.

This process gives the person the much sought after and much needed experience of being listened to, valued as a person and their journey understood.

Other outcomes from the staff perspective have been a better understanding of ways in which a person's needs can be met in relation to activities on the ward, insight having been gained as to what would be 'meaningful' for that person to be involved in.

From the chaplain's perspective there has been much of value. Many insights have been gained from conversations initiated either by the chaplain or by the persons themselves, thus providing a much fuller picture of those involved in the groups: insights that indicate points or issues requiring follow-up; insights that provide a better understanding of the person's behaviours or attitudes. Most importantly it has enabled the 'conversation' to move to another deeper level – one that for the person concerned has real significance.

CHAPTER 12

Eastern Perspectives and Implications for the West

Krishna Mohan

Ageing: a brief introduction

In the last few decades the ageing population has been on the rise throughout the world, especially in the west. In recent years this has led to greater emphasis upon research on ageing. Research on older adults in the past was done more in the areas of illness and health. However, in recent years the focus has shifted to the quality of life and well-being of the aged.

Healthy ageing

The major objective of present-day ageing research is to ensure healthy ageing and longevity. In recent years research evidence does indicate that moderate lifestyle changes not only improve the quality of life but also increase longevity. Longevity research with individuals who lived longer than average in different regions has shown that:

- they eat moderate diets featuring vegetables and herbs and small amounts of meat and fat
- they continue working throughout life
- integration into intergenerational families and community activities occurs
- exercise and relaxation are a part of the daily routine. (Pitskhelauri 1982)

The fact that the human body ages over the years can be understood in terms of primary ageing, due to intrinsic biogenetic processes of ageing, and of secondary ageing, due to external factors such as abuse or disuse of the body, which leads to various diseases and disabilities and is often controllable (Cohen 1988).

Social stereotypes

From a social perspective ageing research has shown that, when compared to other age groups, society has more rigid stereotypes towards the older adult population. Two dominant images persist – a negative image of declining abilities and opportunities and a positive image of increasing wisdom and fortitude – although there tends to be more emphasis upon negative over positive stereotypes. Hebb's (1978) study asked four well-known individuals about their experiences of old age. They stated that:

- they were surprised at being old
- they had to deal with cognitive and physical problems
- they looked for meaning in their lives
- they believed in the value of wisdom and the experience of a long life.

Cultural differences

Cultural differences are one of the important aspects in viewing elderly people. The modernisation theory states that pre-industrial societies accord more status to the aged than industrial societies, and this has been confirmed by research. Ishii-Kuntz and Lee (1987) noted that high status is given to elderly in societies where conformity is highly valued when compared to societies that emphasise self-reliance. Societies with ancestor worship show higher status for the elderly than do other societies. Nusberg (1983) observed that in some societies younger persons are legally expected to provide care for older persons. Moreover, extended families in all cultures exhibit higher status for the elderly.

Personal well-being

Focus on personal well-being and effective living in ageing research is only a recent development. Long, Anderson and Williams (1990) identified six major themes in this connection:

1. The primary contributors to a sense of well-being throughout life are family, religion and good health.

2. Older adulthood is more satisfying than either young adulthood or middle adulthood.

3. The greatest accomplishments in life are successful rearing of children, successful marriages, careers, and religious choices.

4. If older adults could change something about their earlier life, they would get more education or use their education better.

5. Older adults' most important advice to younger people was to live by higher religious or moral principles.

6. As they get older, adults worry less about money, viewing life as intrinsically precious.

Religious faith and activity

Other studies have discovered that the activities bringing the highest satisfaction levels to the older adults studied are informal ones involving friends and family, and that persons over the age of 65 value religion more than younger individuals. Such studies have shown an increase in religious faith, prayer, Bible reading, listening to religious programmes, and spirituality among the elderly (Achenberg 1985; George 1988; Schick 1986; Ward 1984). With regard to the spiritual values and religious activities of older adults, it has been found that 82 per cent have religious faith and regard it as the most important influence in life; for 87 per cent religion gave personal comport and support; and for 89 per cent religious beliefs are put into practice (Gallup 1982).

However, three issues have frequently arisen in the discussions concerning spirituality among elderly persons. The first is the contention that religious beliefs and behaviours increase during the adult years. The second is that religious beliefs mitigate a person's fear (Hood et al. 1996;

Spilka, Hood and Gorsuch 1985). The third, regarding correspondence between religious belief and self-reported religious behaviour, is not clear.

Mental health

In recent years there has been a growing awareness among health professionals of the potential physical and mental health benefits associated with spirituality and religion, especially for older adults. Though spirituality is as much a part of human experience as any other normal form of thought and behaviour, to date it has not been given the attention it deserves by researchers and practitioners in psychology or in mental health (Adams 1995; Canda 1995; Ganje-Fling and McCarthy 1996; Hall 1995; Kane, Cheston and Green 1993; King, Speck and Thomas 1995; Lindgren and Coursey 1995; Pargament 1996; Sargent 1989; Sinclair 1993; Vesti and Kastrup 1995; Weaver, Koeing and Ochberg 1996; Wulff 1996). Mental health professionals in fact have often viewed spiritual content as pathological (Larson *et al.* 1993; Post 1992; Weaver *et al.* 1996).

Persistence of religion

Both religion and spirituality are widespread – indeed universal – phenomena, in that they are integral to all cultures and influence people of all ages, socio-economic status and educational levels. They continue to thrive because of, among other things, social influences and need satisfaction. Particularly in the east, every aspect of life is more or less imbued with either religious sentiments or perceived as part of religious life. There are also revealing statistics from the USA where it is estimated that 94 per cent of the population believe in God; 88 per cent believe God loves them; 81 per cent believe we will be called before God on Judgement Day; 71 per cent believe in life after death; and more people have confidence in organised religion than in any other social institution (Gallup and Castelli 1989). National surveys conducted by the Princeton Religious Research Center indicate that 76 per cent of older Americans rate religion as very important in their lives (Princeton Religious Research Center 1994).

The aim of this chapter is to show research-based evidence that spirituality or a spiritual way of life has a bearing on older adults' well-being. Latterly, an attempt is made to draw implications for the west from the ideas or concepts drawn from eastern spirituality, particularly from Hindu and Buddhist spiritual philosophy, for the well-being of older adults in the twenty-first century.

Spirituality: definition

Definition of spirituality in relevant literature usually includes some version of the following words and phrases: feeling connected or belonging in the universe, believing in a power outside of one's self, searching for a sense of meaning or purpose, experiencing transcendence and immanence, seeking one's ultimate and personal truths, experiencing a numinous quality, knowing unity of the visible and invisible, having an internalised relationship between the individual and the divine, encountering limitless love, and moving towards personal wholeness (Canda 1995; Decker 1993; Ganje-Fling and McCarthy 1996; King *et al.* 1995; Wulff 1996).

However, Reese (1997) strips the term 'spirituality' to its minimally necessary elements and defines it as 'consistency of action with belief'. He argues that spirituality is, in behaviour-analytic terms, rule-governed behaviour in that the rule (belief) that governs this behaviour (action) is a part of a coherent system that defines 'rightness'.

Spirituality and religion

Though spirituality traditionally has been considered exclusively the domain of religion, it is now being conceptualised in terms that have no particular relationship to theology, while at the same time being accepted as practical and intellectually respectable. Worthington *et al.* (1996) speak of three categories while differentiating the religious from the spiritual:

- those who may be spiritual but not religious in that they believe in and value a universal human spirit or an 'élan vital' without holding religious beliefs to be true

- those who are religious but not spiritual holding to the doctrines of a religious organisation but not experiencing any devotion to a higher power

- those who are both spiritual and religious and believe in valuing a higher power that is acceptable to and consistent with some organised religion.

Transcendence

Spirituality that has always been considered as a natural part of being human may be regarded as an innate human capacity to transcend the egocentric perspective from which people constantly experience and evaluate their lives, opening to a broader world view, a heightened capacity for loving and an increased motivation to enhance the greater good. The definition of spirituality provided by the tenth edition of the *Oxford English Dictionary* is as follows: 'the quality or condition of being spiritual, attachment to or regard for the things of the spirit as opposed to material or wordly interest'.

The term 'spirituality' can therefore be said to refer to the individual's experience of a dimension of power and meaning, transcendent to the ordinary sensory reality. According to Vrinte (1996) spirituality is inspired and sustained by transpersonal experiences that originate in the deepest recesses of the human being and they are but the natural manifestations of that domain of the human psyche that contain the greater depth of life.

Krippner and Welch (1992) say that the word 'spiritual' is used to describe aspects of human behaviour and experience that reflect an alleged transcendent intelligence or process, and is associated with several identifiable values:

- *the transcendent dimension*: conceptualised as a supreme being, a 'greater self', or simply as 'something more' from which a person derives a sense of personal power
- *meaning in life*: when an authentic meaning and purpose in life fills an 'existential vacuum'
- *mission in life*: where there is a purpose in one's vocation which may be felt as a 'call' or 'destiny to fulfil'
- *sacredness of life*: where life is not divided into sacred and the secular but all experience is sacralised and suffused with awe and reverence

- *ultimate satisfaction*: a person may take pleasure in material things but the ultimate basis for their happiness and satisfaction lies in spiritual values
- *altruism*: which propels one to respond to the needs of others as connectedness between all persons is felt
- *idealism*: where a commitment is felt to the betterment of the world not only through meditation and prayer but also through concrete actions
- *realism*: where facts of tragedy, suffering, pain or death deepen one's appreciation of life and strength of commitment to make a difference in the world
- *fruits of spirituality*: such as compassion, courage, joy or devotion which have positive effects not only on the spiritual person but also on others and the world around them
- *therapeutic effect*: that draws others to the spiritual person and is viewed by friends as an empowering resource in relationships.

Further, Krippner and Welch (1992) distinguish spirituality from religiosity and maintain that spiritual people may or may not engage in formal religious practice and religious people may not embody spiritual values. They argue that people who have internalised an institutionalised common set of beliefs, practices and rituals (as dictated by religion) regarding spiritual concerns and issues are not always spiritual. This view is elaborated by Vrinte (1996) who says spirituality is distinct from religion in that spirituality is more related to authentic mystical experiences whereas religion is more associated with normative practices (laid down by a prophet or a religious group). In fact Keen (1994) observes that millions of people, who are unmoved by established religion as well as disillusioned with a secular view of life, are looking for some 'missing value', some absent purpose, some 'new meaning' and some 'presence of the sacred' – all of which indicate becoming spiritual in one's orientation.

Spiritual development

Attempts to define spirituality as an innate characteristic that develops in a manner roughly corresponding to psychological development – as defined, for example, by Erikson and Erikson (1982) who said that normal crises precipitated by external or internal changes of life send us from one stage of psychological development to the next – have led Fowler (1981) to propose six stages of spiritual development:

1. Around age two to seven when a child's spirituality is fantasy based.

2. School age when belief becomes more literal and concrete as in seeing God as anthropomorphic.

3. Adolescence governed by the community aspect of spirituality.

4. Early twenties when individuals tend to relocate authority within themselves and rely mostly on rationality.

5. Midlife when there is a shift towards a concept of God as a cosmic flow of life or light within.

6. Finally one reaches the stage of universalising faith with a devotion to a transcendent vision not of one's own making.

Summary

From the above discussion spirituality may be understood as an innate human capacity to transcend the egocentric perspective from which people experience and evaluate their lives and in the process attain full enlightenment: thoughts, feelings of connectedness with the universe, moving towards personal wholeness experiencing transcendence and immanence. Further, spiritual health/well-being may be understood as involving high levels of faith, commitment and behaviour relating to a well-defined worldview or belief system that provides a higher sense of meaning and purpose to existence in general, and that offers an ethical path to personal fulfilment which includes connectedness with self, others and a higher power or larger reality.

Spirituality: eastern and western perspectives

As we have seen, spirituality is not a simple concept. It is used to describe different realities that may have converging elements. One general way of categorising spirituality is into eastern and western forms.

Western spirituality

Spirituality in the west is largely influenced by Christianity which is centred in the concepts of sin and redemption. Further, it tends to be dualistic and to focus on dichotomies: between spirit and matter, body and soul, sacred and profane, heaven and earth, and so on. Another important aspect of the western form of spirituality is understanding salvation as abstract and other worldly. Moreover, its form of prayer is oral and mental, and it is discursive rather than meditative in practice. The emphasis is more on striving for perfection, asceticism, abnegation and self-control.

Eastern spirituality

In contrast eastern spirituality takes a cosmic rather than a personal view of God. It is holistic and emphasis is placed on the oneness of body and soul, matter and spirit, and seeing that the whole universe is interwoven. Further, life's contradictions are seen not as mutually cancelling each other but as two poles of one reality, one giving meaning to the other. Eastern spirituality is creation-centred, ecological and cosmic, conscious of one's interconnectedness with all living beings. The focus of eastern spirituality is on contemplation, silence and intuitive prayer, and it pays attention to bodily posture in prayer and emphasises the role of the guru or spiritual teacher. The main difference from the western spirituality is that eastern spirituality is less pragmatic and, though not denigrating 'doing', it focuses more on 'being' and 'becoming'. The uniqueness of eastern spirituality is that it does not personalise God but goes beyond the father–mother image. Furthermore, salvation is understood as the experience of enlightenment and oneness with the infinite.

Well-being: eastern and western perspectives

Since recorded history, philosophers always considered happiness to be the highest good and ultimate motivation for human functioning, but it is only recently that excellent reviews of the history and philosophy of happiness have begun to appear in psychological literature (Chekola 1975; Culberson 1977; Diener *et al.* 1999; Wilson 1967).

Western perspectives

While there have been many attempts to describe psychological health in ideal terms giving us a list of qualities that go to make a mature, healthy, fully functioning, self-actualising person, it is important to examine definitions provided by some health psychologists who have, in their attempts to define a healthy individual, spelt out a list of specific characteristics, mostly based on research and observation, that could be associated with an individual who is psychologically healthy and experiences a state of well-being most of the time.

In her analysis of many definitions Jahoda (1958) says positive mental health is based on the following:

- attitudes towards the self which include accessibility of the self to consciousness, correct self-concept, one's sense of identity and the acceptance of one's self

- growth, development and self-actualisation

- integration

- autonomy

- perception of reality

- environmental mastery which includes abilities to work, love and play, adequate interpersonal relationships, meeting situational requirements, adaptation and adjustment, and efficiency in problem solving.

David Seedhouse (1995) introspects that the term 'well-being' as used in present-day health promotion literature is an extremely vague notion. While psychologists believe well-being is constructed out of the three components of life-satisfaction, positive affect and negative affect (Diener 1984; Diener *et al.* 1999; Myers and Diener 1995), Seedhouse concludes that judgements of well-being are irreducibly subjective and that the meaning and content of the term are seen to fluctuate, depending on who is using it and why it is being used.

Based on the above discussion, an operational definition of well-being may include the following:

1. It may be understood as a scientific sounding term for what people usually mean by happiness.

2. It refers to what people think and how they feel about themselves, i.e. the cognitive and affective conclusions they reach when they evaluate their existence.

3. It involves the individual's entire condition, i.e. the psychological, social and spiritual aspects of one's existence.

4. Well-being is a relative state of affairs – relative to the situation as well as to the values of the particular culture one belongs to, such as the traditional pattern of 'Indianness' which seeks to avoid extremes, maintain equilibrium, have good health, practise self-control, and arrive at self-realisation and the dissolution of the self.

Eastern perspectives

Indian thought is one of the influential philosophies in the world. The eastern concept of well-being is mainly drawn from Indian thought. The schools of Hindu philosophy are abundant with rich, insightful, psychological treatises on well-being. Buddhism and Jainism each represent a view of personality and describe methods for its growth into a particular form of perception. The various schools of yoga prescribe methods to help reach a high level of consciousness and go beyond the limits of ordinary human experience. Well-being is equated with integration of personality. In summary, psychological well-being to the Hindu means:

- integration of emotions with the help of an integrated teacher (a spiritual master, or guru)
- acquiring a higher philosophy of life which helps to resolve inner tensions
- channelling basal passion by directing the emotions to ultimate reality
- developing an attitude whereby everything is viewed as a manifestation of ultimate reality

- cultivation of higher qualities which replace negative qualities
- the practice of concentration. (Sinha 1965)

The ultimate goal in Indian thought goes beyond self-realisation or transcendence and seeks the spiritual pursuit of the highest state of everlasting happiness – *nirvana* or supreme bliss. The ultimate aim is to attain union with the universal self or *moksha* or *nirvana*. The concept of well-being is also elaborated in *charka samhita*, the ancient treatise on the Indian systems of medicine which is called Ayurveda (the treatise on life). According to the *sankhya* philosophy, human personality is a product of the interaction between the spirit (*pursha*) and matter (*prakriti*). The influence of *prakriti* on behaviour is emphasised in terms of the three *gunas* or qualities: the *sattva* or the element of knowledge; *rajas* or principle of activity, which on the affective side is the cause of all painful experiences; and *tamas* or principle of passivity that clouds our intellect, thereby producing ignorance. It is said that the state of *samyavastha* or equilibrium of the three *gunas* is that which holds the secret of an individual's well-being.

Seminal contributions to the concept of well-being have been made by one of the most widely acclaimed religious philosophical text of the Hindus, the *Bhagavad Gita* (1905), which focuses on the idea of avoidance of extremes and maintaining a kind of balance or equilibrium to enjoy a state of well-being. The concept of well-being in Indian (Hindu) thought is significantly characterised by a state of 'good-mind' which is peaceful, quiet and serene. The *Bhagavad Gita* speaks of steadiness of mind (*sthita pragya*) and performing one's duties without being lustfully attached to the fruits of one's action (*karmayogi*) as representing a healthy person. The dissolution of the self or ego is considered the most evolved stage of mental health. Further it is believed that the healthy mind acts but does not react, and therefore is always watchful of the root cause of any disturbance. A mind which is free from conflicts and hence is clear about its duties which are performed as a spiritual mission is a mind which enjoys well-being (Verma 1998).

Besides 'the steadiness of mind' which is characterised by calm and poise in all situations adverse or favourable, other features such as being friendly, not bearing ill-will towards anyone, compassion, forgiveness, being free from attachment and egoism, and being balanced in both pleasure and pain are hallmarks of well-being according to the *Bhagavad Gita*

(1905, XII.13). Self-realisation, which is the realisation that everything is totally interconnected, and the dissolution of the self by expansion of the self beyond its personal boundary, leads to the finest stage of human life where there are positive feeling for all things and beings. So, according to the Indian thinking, well-being unfolds at cognitive (rigorous self-examination), conative (performance of duty) and affective (expression of self beyond the ego) levels.

Summary

From the above account it is clear that there exist differences about the concept of well-being in the west and the east, in that the conceptualisations made in the west revolve around the ability to satisfy one's needs, avoidance of frustrations and stress, and exercising certain amounts of control on the environment such that it enhances the satisfaction of personal and social needs. In the Indian tradition control over the senses is thought to be essential to well-being. Emphasis is on the maintenance of balance between extremes of satisfaction and denial (implying that needs need not be totally denied) and the adoption of a path of moderation. Further, since frustrations and failures as well as successes and joys are considered inevitable in one's life, the essence of well-being lies in not being overwhelmed by either aspect. While in the west the idea is to have control over or exploit the environment since it is thought to provide the inputs that lead to need satisfaction, in Hindu spiritual thought the concept of 'being in tune' with the environment is encouraged in order to experience well-being.

Research studies

Research on spirituality and well-being has shown a close link (Mohan 2001). Other studies have also shown a salutary effect of spirituality on late life well-being (McFadden 1995). For the purpose of this review of research relating spirituality with well-being, studies involving religious influence have also been considered as they are closely related to spirituality. Religiosity and spirituality were formerly used almost interchangeably but spirituality seems a more inclusive and abstract concept than religiosity (Mahoney and Graci 1999).

Spirituality and health

In recent years there has been growing evidence to suggest the relationship between spirituality and healing in medicine with reference to the major world religions. Culligan's (1996) report of a 1995 conference at Harvard University reflects this new collaborative work between religion and medicine in which there is a recognition of the impact of religion and spiritual practices in health and well-being.

Westgate (1996) in her review proposed four dimensions of spiritual wellness:

- meaning in life
- intrinsic value
- transcendence
- spiritual communality.

Her paper also discussed the implications of these dimensions for research, counselling and counsellor education.

The few studies that investigated well-being measures, spirituality and spiritual experience have found that people who have had spiritual experiences are in the normal range of well-being and have a tendency to report more extreme positive feelings than others (Kennedy and Kanthamani 1995; Kennedy, Kanthamani and Palmer 1994).

In a study by De Rogario (1997) a content analysis was made of 35 lived experience informants and 14 autobiographers who represented a wide range of people with physical disability and chronic illness. It was found that the combined elements of spiritual transformation, hope, personal control, positive social support and meaningful energetic life enabled individuals to improve themselves and come to terms with their respective conditions. These experiences led many people to find a sense of wholeness and unity and to experience and integrate a deeper meaning, sense of self and spirituality within their lives.

In the last few years, investigators in the rapidly growing field of mind–body medicine are coming across findings that suggest that an attitude of openness to such unusual experiences as spiritual, transcendental, peak and mystical may be conducive to health and well-being. For example, Dean Ornish, a heart disease researcher, believes that 'opening your heart' to 'experience a higher force' is an important component of his programme for reversing heart disease (Ornish 1990, Chapter 9).

Religion, faith and well-being

There are other studies that relate illness and spirituality as Reese (1997) found in her study of terminally ill adults aged 20 to 85 years:

1. They had a greater spiritual perspective than non-terminally ill hospitalised adults and healthy non-hospitalised adults.

2. Their spiritual perspective was positively related to well-being.

3. A significantly larger number of terminally ill adults indicated a change towards increased spirituality than did non-terminally ill or healthy adults.

Numerous studies have found positive relationships between religious beliefs and practices and physical or mental health measures. Although it appears that religious belief and participation may possibly influence one's subjective well-being, many questions need to be answered such as when and why is religion related to psychological well-being. Worthington *et al.* (1996) in their review offer some tentative answers to why religion may sometimes have positive effects on individuals. Religion may:

- produce a sense of meaning, something worth living and dying for (Spilka, Shaver and Kirkpatrick 1985)
- stimulate hope (Scheier and Carver 1987) and optimism (Seligman 1991)
- give religious people a sense of control by a beneficient God, which compensates for reduced personal control (Pargament *et al.* 1987)
- prescribe a healthier lifestyle that yields positive health and mental health outcomes
- set positive social norms that elicit approval, nurturance and acceptance from others
- provide a social support network
- give the person a sense of the supernatural that is certainly a psychological boost – but may also be a spiritual boost that cannot be measured phenomenologically (Bergin and Payne 1993).

It is also reported by Myers and Diener (1995) that people who experience sustained levels of happiness are more likely to say that they have a meaningful religious faith than people who are not happy over a long period of time.

A study by Hadway (1978) on religiosity concluded that religion is one potential resource in people's lives. More recently Myers and Diener (1995) in their survey of related studies observe that links between religion and mental health are impressive and that culture and religiosity may provide better clues to understanding the nature of well-being. Religious belief and practice play an important role in the lives of millions of people worldwide. The review by Selway and Ashman (1998) highlighted the potential of religion to affect the lives of people with disability, their families and care-givers.

Religious coping

Research relating stress to religion indicated that religious and non-religious people tend to experience equal amounts of stress but religion may help people deal better with negative life events and attendant stress (Schafen and King 1990). Maton's study (1989) supports the view that individuals with high levels of stress are likely to benefit from perceived spiritual support, and this is consistent with the coping model based on religion proposed by Pargament (1996). In a study by Williams *et al.* (1991) of 720 adults religious attendance buffered the deleterious effects of stress on mental health. Courtenary *et al.* (1992) found a significant relationship between religiosity and physical health and that religion and coping were strongly related especially among the oldest old.

With regard to coping Pargament (1996) cites five studies which show that religious forms of coping are especially helpful to people in uncontrollable, unmanageable or otherwise difficult situations. Along the same lines Moran (1990) also believes that survivors may benefit by experiencing God as a refuge and as a reason to have hope. Patricia (1998) in her review shows how religion and spirituality helps adult survivors of childhood violence.

Individuals with strong religious faith have been found to report higher levels of life satisfaction, greater personal happiness and fewer negative psychological consequences of traumatic life events (Ellison, Gey and

Glass 1991). Anson, Antonovsky and Sagy (1990) examined among 639 Jewish retirees over 60 years the relationship between self-rated religiosity, physical and psychological well-being and life satisfaction using data from a longitudinal study. Findings revealed religiosity was only weakly and inversely related to health and psychological distress, and that decline in well-being during the follow-up year led to an increase in religiosity. Ellison's (1993) data from a national survey of Black Americans supported the hypothesis that participation in church communities fosters positive self-perception. Mookherjee's (1994) study found that perception of well-being was positively and significantly influenced by, amongst other things, church membership and frequency of church attendance.

Intrinsic and extrinsic religion

Many psychologists who study religion distinguish between intrinsic and extrinsic religious orientation (Paloutzian 1996). An intrinsic orientation involves internal religious motives within a person. By contrast extrinsic orientation involves external motives outside the religion, using the religion for non-religious ends. There appears to be a positive correlation between intrinsically religious people (religion as an end in itself) deriving substantial positive mental health benefit from their religion (Donahue 1985). Intrinsic religiosity has been related to the following qualities characterising positive mental health: internal locus of control, intrinsic motivational traits, sociability, sense of well-being, responsibility, self-control, tolerance, and so on (Bergin 1991).

A longstanding misconception is that religion is a crutch for the weak. However, researchers in the psychology of religion have found that many religious individuals were competent. Payne *et al.* (1991) in their review on religion and mental health found that there was a positive influence of intrinsic religiosity on mental health in regard to well-being. In one study Ventis (1995) found that individuals with intrinsic religious motivation reported a greater sense of competence and control, as well as less worry and guilt, when compared with individuals with extrinsic religious motivation. From the compelling evidence based on the literature it can be said that spirituality and religion are a potent force in society, shaping both individuals and institutions.

Conclusion and implications

Encouraging developments

Spirituality and religion, despite their significance for individuals and institutions, have been neglected by psychologists and other mental health professionals for most of the last century. In more recent years, however, there have been signs of renewed interest in the study of spirituality and religion. In the earlier history of psychology there have been many influential thinkers in the field who have included religion or spirituality in their theories, e.g. Freud, James, Jung, Erikson and Maslow (Wulff 1996). But this gradually faded out with the rise of behaviourism as a legitimate and respected field of study for psychologists (Dennis 1995).

Recent years however have witnessed encouraging developments in research interest in the interaction of spirituality and mental health, and this is currently growing (Adams 1995; Hall and Hall 1997; Wulff 1996). Another encouraging sign in this direction is that recent psychiatric literature and contemporary socio-political developments are suggesting a need to reconsider political developments and the place of religion and spirituality in psychiatry (Turbott 1996).

Further, it appears that science and spirituality are no longer considered as being diametrically opposed or mutually exclusive (Neil 1995). For example, Helminiak (1996) argues that spirituality can meet the demanding criteria that qualify it as a science, as a specialisation within psychology. There is also a renewed effort in psychology to embrace spirituality (Dennis 1995) and a recognition that it was a serious oversight to have ignored for so many years the role of spirituality in the development of the psyche (Gopaul-McNicol 1997).

Given its concern with the individual-in-context and the rapid changes in the modern world, spirituality has many implications for mental health in particular and psychology in general. Further, considering religion/spirituality as a cultural phenomenon which has relevance and meaning for its practitioners, it cannot be understood in a secular frame drawn from the west. It opens a new area of significant study in understanding human dynamics of non-European cultures. It also holds the key to understanding the behaviour patterns and modes of thought which westerners often find either amusing or puzzling.

Implications for therapy

The need for mental health professionals to be sensitised to the role of religion and spirituality as coping mechanisms is being stressed (Jenkins and Pargament 1995) and many believe that spiritual approaches may be appropriate for inclusion in therapy if the client and situation warrant it (Kivley 1986). On the same lines Ross (1994) argues that understanding and judicious encouragement of religious practice can augment therapy and provide a basis for reframing, which can assist in treatment. Sappington (1994) calls for the development of a psychology of Christian living to help in Christian-oriented counselling.

In fact a wide range of spiritual healing traditions emphasise the central importance of the connection of all life to spiritual or cosmic realities. In these views, healing is usually seen as restoring a condition of wholeness or harmony (Carlson and Shield 1989). Several investigators have studied the relative frequency of use of various religious techniques in counselling and psychotherapy. For example, Ball and Goodyear (1991) found that prayer has often been used by religious counsellors for religious clients as an adjunct to counselling. In a study by Soderton and Martinson (1987) it was found that 25 cancer patients' main strategy for coping with cancer was through prayer.

Indian insights

Keeping in view the Indian perspective of spirituality and well-being and the link between religion/spirituality and well-being has many implications for ageing. The insights drawn from Indian spirituality can enrich western understanding of well-being. Further, it can help people to move from a materialist-based life towards a more spiritual one. From a broader perspective it helps people to move away from self-centred individualism towards a recognition of the fundamental wholeness and interconnectedness of human beings. An integration of eastern perspective with western understanding can enrich the field of geriatrics, with specific reference to ageing, spirituality and well-being in the twenty-first century.

CHAPTER 13

Ageist Theology

Some Pickwickian Prolegomena

Kevin Barnard

Introduction

The development of *theologies of...* has often been linked with the isolation of a problem or set of problems. For example, it would be arguable that there would be no need for a theology of work if work were not the occasion of certain problems.

It is because of this tendency that I should venture to resist any attempt to speak of a *theology of ageing*. In short, such a label might be taken as suggesting that ageing is to be treated as a problem. Of course, there are problems that arise in connection with ageing, but perhaps these very problems are problems of society, and the ageing process is a way by which the Word of God is pointing to failure in society. There are problems for people facing dementia or debilitating illness, problems which call for a 'theodicy' or vindication of what God has allowed to come about. Nonetheless such problems are, theologically, no different from the problems confronting other sufferers. However, ageing in itself is not to be seen as a problem demanding a theology.

This is part of the reason for the title of this chapter. 'Ageism', of course, is seen as discrimination or injustice springing from judgements based purely upon age. In that way, 'ageism' is comparable to 'sexism'. However, this chapter seeks to align the word more with 'feminism', in order to see the positive in the ageing process.

This different use of the word 'ageist' is thus 'Pickwickian', a word commandeered for the purposes of this chapter. But also, just as Mr Pickwick and his friends garnered miscellaneous information, so this chapter brings together a few odd points to explore how the study of ageing may learn from and contribute to theology. (The rest of the title is simply explained – anything with prolegomena must be serious!)

Theology and ageing

If there are problems associated with ageing, there are also resources for church and community, politics and theology available because of ageing. It is seen as impossible for any single theologian to be competent in all areas of theology. This means that doing theology is an exercise in collaboration. The church's memory, its experience and its discernment are to be the resources for assessing theological studies and relating them to each other. But the church can only carry out this task because of its age, its maturity and its informed judgement, even when maturity demands that we become like children, for age gives the confidence to do so. It is the adolescent, not the adult, who shrinks from childlikeness.

Again, theology must be concerned with the ageing of the church in its relations with an ageing world of thought. Just as many of the social issues around human ageing have to do with communication and participation, so much theological debate has been about communication and participation. How is the Christian message to be expressed and communicated? How is Christianity to participate in the intellectual and opinion-forming realms?

If we may use one of the problems of ageing to illustrate the problems of Christian theology, we have the issue of *identity*. Those who frequently have contact with older people (especially persons who develop dementia) know that the retention of identity is a serious issue. How is the identity of Christianity to be maintained or discerned in the journey from Jerusalem through Rome and Nicaea to …Geneva? …Oxford? …the streets of Brazil or Soweto? …the national elegance and pageantry of Westminster Abbey or the worship of a metropolitan community church?

Here the church and the ageing human being face comparable questions and the answer for both might be found in the philosophical response of bodily and mental continuity, the continuing relatedness of faculty to faculty, the location of the individual within a community or family (comparable to the location of the Christian community within a community of communities all going through their own evolution) and the use of reminiscence, which has always been a resource for the individual Christian and the whole Christian community.

If *theology of ageing* is a difficult (or even dangerous) term, it is still worthwhile to bring the two together and speak of theology *and* ageing, for in all these words one very basic question has to be: What is the difference between *ageing* and *living*? If theology and life are to be kept in dialogue, theology and ageing cannot avoid one another.

Ageing as process

To live is to age. Of course, to age is not necessarily to live, but people's mixed feelings about ageing can be understood in part if we think of the difference between the ageing of a wine and the ageing of a cheese. Within the human ageing process there is a 'wine side' and a 'cheese side'. Just as cheeses go off after a relatively short time, while some wines improve over a relatively long time, so people often feel both improvement and deterioration come with ageing.

But we still need to ask: What is the difference between living and ageing? Most obviously, living is a process *and* the condition of all other processes, whereas ageing is the way our 'doing living' varies through time. Ageing thus incorporates learning, growing and practising, as well as slowing or being impaired or finding something no longer worthwhile or rewarding. Such a distinction incorporates both the 'wine' and the 'cheese' sides.

The idea of process, however, takes us to the doctrines of humanity and of God. In his book *In Search of Humanity*, John Macquarrie writes:

> 'Nature' is derived from *naturus*, the future participle of the Latin verb *nasci*, 'arise', 'be born'. *Natura* is that which is arising or coming to birth and the nature of the human being, the as yet unfinished humanity which is emerging and taking shape in the history of the race and in the existence of each individual... We now see from our consideration of the word 'nature' that this study [that is, of human nature] is concerned with something that is fluid, coming to be and always on the move. (Macquarrie 1982, p.3)

Ageing is about changing. We can, therefore, recognise in the ageing process the manifestation of human nature, human becoming.

Communal ageing

There has been communal ageing also. While it is often urged that many of the important elements of life – relating, striving, hunger, celebration, etc. – have lasted through the centuries, nevertheless our ways of viewing ourselves and the world, descended though they are from the thought forms of earlier generations, are different from the worldview of our ancestors. Although the question 'Are we the same as people of 2000 years ago?' is important in such matters as the use of the Bible, of more importance for our present subject is the very fact that the question can be asked, for it points to awareness of human change together with awareness of uncertainty (possibly *collective* awareness) as to the depth or extent of that change. The very existence of the process is a form of identity and, though the acorn of 1800 might not be recognisable by the observer of the oak of 2000, there is continuity.

Communal ageing is not about ceasing to be. It is rather about the cumulative shaping of a direction, a direction which is not the result of the growth of one self-contained unit, but is the chart of the relations between each unit and all the units so far, any of which might have an impact (as we learn from genetics) on the life of the total organism. A comparison can be drawn with music. Any person's or group's life can be regarded as a piece of music and the exact value of each note or chord is not known until the end.

Past and future

With respect to the community (and the individual), this means that the past is never definitely dead. The past is carried up into the present and the present is the means of access to the past. This means that the past – of the individual, the community, the church, the race – is essential in the process of evaluating and understanding, for each moment (whether present or future) must be assessed eventually by its quality as *the past*.

This interlocking of moments as parts of a process has important ethical implications. There has been much debate about the importance of 'possible people' in the formation of policy decisions, for it has been argued that as future people do not exist they cannot be harmed and so need not be borne in mind now. However, 'honour your great-grandchildren' is a corollary of honouring your father and mother, for if you do not honour them you are implying that the process to which you are now contributing, the past which you are becoming, is of no value.

Ageing and theology, especially here moral theology, bear on one another. We do not age in isolation. The sorrows and achievements of each generation do not become immediately apparent and, just as a full account of someone's actions must take account of space (the impact of an act can be felt within a room, a village, a nation and the world), so one's actions remain one's own throughout the course of time. In ageing as individuals we contribute to the ageing (the living) of the race and the groups to which we belong. There is a comparability of time and space in these questions, for, however small the distance between two people, there is a lapse of time between one's acting and the other's being affected, so that the person of the subsequent time, affected by the action, might be said not to exist.

Without being rigid determinists, we can see how the present state of the race (or the church or community) is the product of the past, each phase of which has an influence on the present. (In this way, as in several others, an analogy between individual and group ageing is possible and illuminating.) Just as the life of the individual is not to be considered of more or less value in itself according to the individual's age, so the life of the race is not to be seen as becoming more or less valuable as time passes. (Bearing in mind Macquarrie's words quoted above, perhaps we can say that the human race does not become *more* human with the passage of time, but rather that our humanity is *in* the becoming.)

To look down on the standards of a previous age is to ignore the fact that we should not enjoy or maintain our present standards were it not for the experiments (moral as well as material) of previous ages and the fact that there will be that in our present age which will make us the objects of the pity and the censure of succeeding generations.

The corporate dimension

Modesty, then, is to be encouraged. This is not the (often false) modesty of the relativist who would deny that we can talk of improvement. Rather, it is a modesty based upon the sense of the corporate which is a major part of the Judaeo-Christian tradition. Resisting both individualism and collectivism, it is possible to use the idea of the corporate nature of humanity, drawing on the treatment of the relationship between the individual and the community in the Old Testament and in the New, looking not only to Saint Paul's use of the body image in 1 Corinthians but also to such passages as John 15:1–11 and parts of Colossians in which creation itself as well as the church are treated in a way that uses body imagery.

Just as different parts of our bodies age at different rates, so we may use the body image to remind ourselves that different parts of the body which is humanity age at different rates and memories stored in one part of the body are accessible to the whole body. So caution is needed as we avoid the idolatry of modernity or the idolatry of the past. If we treat the past as living, we can be delivered from idolatry around it. But such an expression as 'the living past' raises its own difficulties.

Different kinds of 'past'

In one sense, the past is fixed. Nothing can alter the fact that the Battle of Hastings took place in 1066 or that I drank tea at breakfast yesterday. It is odd, therefore, to talk of the past as living. Its influence may be felt, but now it is felt like the impact of the throwing of a stone into a pond, an event now over in which the stone takes no further part, whilst what lives in the pond is reacting to the stone.

However, just as 'the present' can be defined in various ways according to the context in which the word is used, so the past impinges in various ways, or even is past for some and not for others. The child at school today may study the Second World War as history, but there are still those for whom it is part of their present. Yet also our grasp of the past changes, and in this sense we still give it life, or it is still present to us and so giving us life, as the importance of events, at all levels, is reassessed, celebrated, forgotten, explained or exploited. It might be said that there are four kinds of past:

1.   There is the *archaeological past*, that which would be visible if we
     travelled in a time machine.

2.   There is the *significant past*, what is now valued or used as a
     point of reference (a *signum*) in explaining or managing the
     present.

3.   There is the *unacknowledged past*, which is often the concern of
     the psychologist, but which should also be the concern of the
     theologian, working as a kind of therapist for the church, and
     of the church working as healing prophet for the world.

4.   These three pasts are related to each other in various ways, but
     there is also the *mythical past*, akin to the significant past but
     subject to interpretation. (The words 'mythical' and 'myth' are
     here used without any pejorative overtones or judgements as to
     the coincidence of the mythical past with the archaeological.)

The mythical past

To understand the distinction between the significant and the mythical we
might look at the way importance is given to events in the past. The Battle
of Waterloo is receding as a piece of the significant past and will eventually
cease to be part of it, though still part of the chain of events by which the
archaeological past is to be explained. However, it might still form part of
the mythical past, perhaps as contributing to views of history based on
class analysis or to militaristic xenophobia.

On the other hand, the mythical past may or may not be related to a
setting in the timescale of the archaeological past but is rather a point of
reference whose meaning is still being explored by the community and
shaping the community's perception. Thus the Greek myths ceased to be
myths once they were relegated to the realm of Kingsley's *The Heroes* or the
notes at the back of school editions of Homer or Virgil, but they became
myths once more when used by Passolini or Anouilh, who both represented them to allow part of their message to be explored and to
understand or give expression to the present. The significant past has its
significance fixed by those who make it significant; the mythical past is
given. It can be a demon (as in the case of the *age of ignorance* from which we

strive to liberate ourselves) or an angel (as in the case of the *age of nobility* to the ideals of which we must seek to conform).

But more than that – and here the ageing of the church is shown – the mythical past is adaptable, for the myth is both the core around which reiteration is woven (and so from which identity is secured) and the narrative and proclamation given in each of the uses of the core. The myth of Christmas is one, and yet through more than a million sermons it has taken new forms in the process by which its truth is explored.

The ageing church

The ageing of the church and the ageing of the individual are comparable. Within any group mythologies and significant pasts are necessary and the individual participates in the group by the 'ownership' of the myth and by subordination to it and acquires her/his significant past as well as using the significant past of the group.

The church has in various ways faced crises in its ageing process similar to those faced by individuals. Challenges to authority, the impact of new knowledge or skills or sciences, and challenges to fundamentalism or literalism are parts of the life of the church and parts of the life of the individual. Fragmentation, the division of the church into denominations or groups, is mirrored in the life of the individual, whether as family drifts apart or friendships end or as life is compartmentalised and the differing compartments yield differing (and competing or conflicting) demands and values. Even the boundaries of identity can be blurred. The individual can ask 'How far do I identify myself with and through this action?' but also the search for the true self can be hard and painful, whilst in acts of heroism or experiences of extreme guilt the individual's identity can be lost or fulfilled in the life of the group.

The church too has its identity crises. What is morally acceptable in the eyes of the world may not be in the eyes of some Christians, but where is *the church* in this? Does the Nicene Creed give a definitive expression in definitive terminology of Christian doctrine or is it an important but time-bound encapsulation of something needing new expression? Denominations and individuals have to come to terms with such issues as they appropriate Christianity and as Christianity comes to bear on their lives. The whole interfaith debate can be as much a threat to identity within faith as psychiatric illness can be a threat to personal identity.

Just as the life of the individual is made up of sections, some separate and some overlapping, through time and at the same time, so the church claims to be one through time, even though it has changed and even though the beliefs and practices of some who claim membership of the church are widely divergent from and even opposed to those of others. All life for the individual is a struggle for integrity. In the individual, such phases or events as adolescence, leaving home, marriage, work, the birth of children, bereavements and retirement can all be stressful and raise the questions: Who am I? How do I fit into the world? What can I expect of life? Comparable questions are asked of the church as it ages.

Again, crises come when the unacknowledged past intrudes. As already said, in the case of the individual the unacknowledged past is generally the concern of the psychologist or psychiatrist, but the unacknowledged past of the church and the western world has emerged especially over the twentieth century and theology has been shaped by confronting it, whilst the church has still a task of helping the world confront its past.

The church coming to terms with its past

In three areas particularly, the past – which has always been there but has been suppressed, denied or accommodated – has had a great impact.

Western and white

Despite great missionary activity, the life and thinking of the institutional church has been normatively white and European and North American. Black and non-European theologies challenge the acceptability of this norm. As someone ages, so s/he, on looking beyond family, can see how certain things taken for granted may not be the only way of behaving or may not even be good. So the ageing church is led to question itself and recover its essence. Only if the church learns to see itself differently can it repent. Only by repentance can it lead the world to repent, as the church is made up of people in the world, experiencing the ageing of society – and seeking to cope with it.

As with any group, the church must cope with its members as they grow, enabling individuals to retain their identities but also benefit from and contribute by their membership. In a comparable way, the church must keep a balance between so identifying with the world as to lose its purpose (that is, become too integrated) and keeping at such a distance from the world that it fails to serve its purpose (that is, being too careful of its integrity). Applying the similitude of the salt (Matthew 5:13) is a never-ending process.

Male

In its form and its proclamation the church has also been a predominantly male institution. The normal language for speaking of God has used male terms and women have been viewed as defective males. The institutionalised classification of women as whores or virgins or mothers (or all three) may stem from fears about sexuality. The encouragement and manipulation of women into the denial of elements of their identity has harmed both women and men.

Today in areas where animism is practised there is also a belief in a great god, and this deity – fundamental also in religions which are not animistic – is asexual. The differentiated pantheon of male and female gods emerged later than fundamental monotheism. The words of Genesis (1:27–8), 'in the image of God he created him; male and female he created them', may be a recovery of the deity worshipped in time past, whose nature justifies no claim of superiority on grounds of gender.

In the ageing process, a healthy integration of all elements of the person is important. Sexuality and gender role are not the same and are sometimes painfully confused. It is a misuse (perhaps a specially *male* misuse) of the title 'feminist theology' to see it as the area for considering sexuality. To say that *the male* is not normative for the concept of humanity means either denying the essential place of gender and sexuality in understanding humanity or accepting that, at a profound level, there is no one pattern of development.

Justice and health are sometimes linked (though not always in an explicitly causal relationship) in the Bible and natural law, and the church must come to terms with its unacknowledged past, as must western society.

Individuals face new courses which may lead to freedom or temptation (or both).

It is a commonplace that sexuality is a developing process, but it has been assumed that at a certain age the process stops. Why? Changes in forms of family life challenge assumptions about gender. What does 'Christian family life' mean? Have men and women both been too ready to hide behind gender roles? Might the church not have something useful to say about *friendship* as a way of moving from the 'genitalising' of all relationships? (On this it would be worthwhile to listen to such as the eleventh century Aelred of Rievaulx.) Might not the sacramentality of sexual activity be explored with greater freedom not simply by the church in deadening official pronouncements but with the encouragement of the church as it entrusts the exploration to couples?

As a way into the church's unacknowledged past this can touch on difficult areas for many. The exposure of fear and of structures of control that is part of a healthy ageing must, however, be pursued within the church. Here the church does not so much have something to say about ageing as have something to learn from the ageing process. Just as the raising of such issues in one area leads both to a critique of church and theology and to a shaping of their agenda, so the third way into the unacknowledged past of the church, as well as bringing to light matters that it would have been superficially more comfortable to conceal, can give new impetus to the theological enterprise.

Exploitative

This third way into the unacknowledged past is the way of liberation theology. Though much of this has come from outside Europe, its starting point is different from that of other non-European theologies. It connects with spirituality and moral and systematic theologies by an examination of the relatedness of humanity to itself and the material order in its actuality, not beginning from an idealised form. This theology 'from below' has been practised at least since the days of the prophet Amos.

Spirituality is questioned if it becomes escapism. There is a difference between resigned love of God and acquiescence in an evil system. Saint Thérèse of Lisieux can seem an odd example of liberation spirituality, but she is a good example of one who sought Jesus, not sanctity, and at terrible cost (Miller 1998; Neame 1997). The sentence in the Anglican funeral service reminding us that we brought nothing into the world and can take nothing out is liberating, for it reminds us that it is the person, not the possessions, that matters to God. This needs to be heard in a society obsessed with possessions.

Yet a distinction between spirituality and ethics needs to be drawn. What this means can be seen by reflecting on John Henry Newman's words:

> God has created me to do Him some definite service; He has committed some work to me which He has not committed to another. I have my mission – I may never know it in this life, but I shall be told it in the next. I am a link in a chain, a bond of connection between persons. He has not created me for naught. I shall do good, I shall do His work. I shall be an angel of peace, a preacher of truth in my own place *while not intending it* – if I do but keep His commandments. Therefore, I will trust Him. Whatever, wherever I am, I can never be thrown away. If I am in sickness, my sickness may serve Him; in perplexity, my perplexity may serve Him; if I am in sorrow, my sorrow may serve Him. He does nothing in vain. He knows what He is about. He may take away my friends, He may throw me among strangers. He may make me feel desolate, make my spirits sink, hide my future from me – still He knows what He is about. (Newman 1893, quoted in Harrold 1943, pp.356–7)

It is dangerous when such words are used to encourage passivity, a mistaken resignation. No one can say them for another. They are a goal, not a programme. As a moral *goal* to be sought by an individual they are the words of a saint. As a moral *programme* they are the words of an ecclesiastical fascist.

The shaping of life by material conditions cannot be denied and much festers, causing hostility and suspicion as the church's past relations with secular powers and possessions are remembered. Theology calls the church to repent. God's healing can work if we take seriously the fact that healing will not come if an individual's sanctity is bought at the cost of dehumanising others. From talk of Adam to talk of being in Christ, Christianity recognises that we are shaped by societal forces, we are not called to rise stoically above them.

At the social level, might we not ground a critique of the individualisation of welfare provision on the image of the body? The capitalist derives profit from services paid for by the employee, such as health care and education. Redistributive taxation, even if it does not achieve the state idealised in Deuteronomy, is still an expression of belonging to one another. *Marginalisation is happening to the elderly.*

Part of the healing of the world is to come through the prophetic therapy of facing the unacknowledged, which includes recognising that we are heirs of the injustices as well as the achievements of our forebears.

The ageing believer

Just as the church's ageing is helped by its coming to terms with its past, so the ageing of each believer is in some ways a microcosm of church history. In her/his life there will be Pentecostal moments, times of crisis and discovery, of reformation (perhaps involving a change of denominational allegiance) and counter-reformation (bringing new appreciation of resources already available to the person in question).

This process may be an illustration of what Robert Slater (1995) describes in *The Psychology of Growing Old*:

> In western society, speed would seem to be a positive attribute, but slowness can have its advantages too… For example, it can afford the chance for a heightened appreciation of nature. In a similar vein, Gadow and Berg [1978]…suggest: 'It may be that with age we realise time has the dimensions of depth as well as duration…we slow ourselves then to explore experiences, not in their linear pattern of succeeding one another, but in their possibility of opening for us entire worlds in each situation and in each person encountered. We slow ourselves to be more gentle with these experiences, to take care to let their possibilities, their rich density emerge.' (Slater 1995, p.56)

In the same book Slater writes of people as acquiring a greater sense of the interconnectedness of things. In this light, might not the artist, novelist or poet – and the prophet – be seen as old before their time, able to show what is already there because of their perception of depth?

In this instance, and even more in liturgy, the church takes worshippers from archaeological time and places them in the timeless mythical past. In liturgy, event takes priority over explanation. The latter happens in archaeological time – and is necessary – but it is the former which endures.

And hope – the transcending of archaeological time in reaching and enjoying the mythic future to which our lives are oriented – also comes (though not exclusively) through liturgy. Hope, paradoxically, enables the acceptance of the unfinished, an attitude at the heart of Hebrews Chapter 11.

The purpose of life

There is often embarrassment around talk of the purpose of life, but if *nature* involves becoming we can use words from both sides of the Reformation to move to the doctrine of God. The Westminster Shorter Catechism begins:

QUESTION 1: What is the chief end of man?

ANSWER: Man's chief end is to glorify God and enjoy Him for ever.

Ignatius Loyola had written 99 years earlier: 'Man has been created to praise, reverence and serve our Lord God, thereby saving his soul' (Loyola 1973, p.22).

Ideas of purpose and process raise questions for human life, but we may see them in a new light and use them in reflection on the teaching that humanity is made in God's image.

The suggestive title of Eberhard Jungel's study of Barth's doctrine of the Trinity is *God's Being is in Becoming* (1976). Becoming is of the essence of God, and in Jesus God became human. The Incarnation is thus a window for us onto the eternal self-love and overflowing love of God. This window enables us to see the three Persons of the Trinity active in a relationship richer than numerical relatedness. Honouring and being honoured, taking, showing, bringing life and fruit are parts of the life of the eternal Trinity.

Human life, made in God's image, can thus accept process and change, the holding together of stages and facets of our lives in one substance which is itself, like energy (in the non-theological sense), subtle and enduring. The mutual dependence of the Persons and the expression of being through each reflect the life of the whole. This may enable the inclusion of disorder in the life of God, as the dementia sufferer's pain is expressed in the cry, 'My self, my self, why have you forsaken me?'

Beyond the individual level, it is arguable that it is humanity that is made in God's image, not individuals. There is no divine common element in all which is the only thing that matters but each has an unique place in the one mosaic which in its totality displays God's image.

The need to return

If becoming is of the essence of God, we may see the frustration or perversion of becoming as defining sin. In the story of Adam and Eve we can see sin as the attempt to deny dependence and to find a false identity (to become like God/gods); that is, to become or grow in the wrong way.

The Trinity shows interdependence as a picture of psychological and social health, which is not burdened with competition or resentment and not finding fulfilment in static equilibrium.

In our religious life, mythic time – to which we have access by prayer and sacrament – makes archaeological time real. In the interplay of grace and freedom we have a pattern for healthy ageing, as the child grows both from and because of parents, and societies age through revolution and rediscovery. In a real sense, the words of Thomas Ken's (1637–1711) hymn are about atonement, the proper relating of ages and stages of life (individual, social or ecclesiastical), as outlined in the earlier treatment of different kinds of theology:

> That with the world, myself and Thee
> I ere I sleep at peace may be.

In the Bible *returning* is an image of salvation and atonement and the use of ritual to put the worshipper in touch with mythic time for initiatory or therapeutic purposes is widespread. The provision of *structure* rather than *meaning* through religious practice deserves to be explored as part of the reason why older people 'cope' with ageing better if they are active in practising the faith they profess. In this part of the chapter I am indebted to Mircea Eliade's work (1965).

The old image of the Golden Age no longer seems to have its power. Recently, *progress* rather than *restoration* has been valued. Nevertheless, for its own sake and for the world's sake, the church must speak of *both/and*, not *either/or*. In the individual and the communal there is healthy remembrance and unhealthy retrogression – integration of the past and denial of it. A healthy (saved) present is only attainable through the healing of the past – repentance.

Fear of the future, another facet of ageing, has to be faced. Origen recognised the possibility of cycles of fall and redemption as a consequence of restoration. Augustine saw salvation as a move from a state of being able not to sin to one of not being able to sin, not because people are reduced to robots but because they are freed to live according to their nature, their purpose, of knowing and loving God. The younger son in Jesus's parable of the Prodigal Son is described as coming to his senses. The healing of the past and the challenge of the future in that parable give us a picture of ageing, especially in such an exposition as that given by Henri Nouwen (1994).

Other images

The city

Integration and development are combined in another biblical image of salvation, that of the city. Protection, social intercourse, and improvement through collaboration are all possible in the city, and should be sought in the cities of the soul and of the church. The city is a place of endless activity, and just as the God who is love is always active so we are called to an endless journey.

An endless journey

Gregory of Nyssa's view of life as an endless journey well balances any obsession with a 'classical' view of perfection as rest. We are on a journey into God. How can that journey end (Musurillo 1961)? The hymn 'New Every Morning' speaks of new visions of the familiar, part of the journey of ageing, the acquisition of depth mentioned by Slater (1995).

Dying and rising

The dying and rising imaged in baptism remind us that what we cannot escape in archaeological time gains meaning through the entry of mythic time in worship. We are to experience ageing in worship (rather than escape) and by that ageing become priests and prophets for a world living in archaeological time.

To live is to age and to age is to die – and not just physically. We are called to die to self, to die daily in order to be born anew. A good treatment of this theme is in one of Austin Farrer's sermons:

> Man's destiny consists of two parts: first we live and then we die. That is a platitude, but the next step isn't a platitude. In the eyes of God our dying is not simply negative, it is an immensely important and salutary thing; by living we become ourselves, by dying we become God's, if, that is, we know how to die; if we so die, that everything we have become in our living is handed back to the God Who gave us life, for Him to refashion and use according to His pleasure... In a perfect Christian life, if we can talk of such a thing, the dying and the living would go on side by side from the start. (Farrer 1960, pp.13–14)

To learn to love is to learn to die to self, and even to die to the image of the neighbour one once loved in order to love one's neighbour more truly; and to die to the image of God one has so far fashioned (or even that has so far been fashioned in one) in order to be brought to that vision of God which is given to the pure in heart. Church, society, the individual – all must go through this process of ageing and dying.

CHAPTER 14

Geriatric Burden
or Elderly Blessing?

David Jenkins

As the current Anglican Patron of the Christian Council on Ageing and a previous Bishop of Durham (from 1984 to 1994) still living near Durham, I was invited to preside at the final Saturday morning sessions of the Second International Conference on Ageing, Spirituality and Well-being. I agreed to attend the seven lectures (called 'keynote addresses' in the programme) to be given during the mornings of the conference, but I did not take part in the afternoon workshops or evening activities. These notes, therefore, do not reflect on the processes or successes of the conference as such or as a whole.

Practitioners and professionals in a common area of human concern and organisation draw – severally and individually – a great deal out of an extended period of meeting with their fellows. I myself found each of the keynote addresses to be of considerable interest. I could tell from the nature of the flow of questions prompted by each session and the buzz that followed them that participants were finding matters of great interest both in these addresses and among themselves. I have to confess, however, that I found the whole conference somehow disquieting and oddly unsatisfactory. By its end I was not sure what it was all about and where, if anywhere, it pointed to for further activity and discussion.

My interest was in whether the conference would show signs of developing (or being related to developing) a momentum for tackling the economic, political and humane issues arising out of the increasing proportion of the 'aged' or the 'ageing' in the community due to the fact that more and more of us are living longer. This shift in society's make-up clearly has fundamental implications for our economic needs and, therefore, for our political concerns and financial requirements, both personally and in respect of the government on behalf of the country at large.

I personally have been involved in both academic and practical discussions about such matters in regard to health services, exploring questions of distribution of doctors and social services. I have been aware for over a decade that if I were to live as long as my father (who remained self-supporting and in good health until well into his ninety-sixth year) I would be part of the biggest geriatric burden this country has ever had to bear.

As well as the economic problems raised by the challenge, I am struck by social symptoms such as the emergence of new medical terms, technology and organisation (let alone drugs, prostheses and so on). A technical medical term derived from Greek is now in currency (which shows that we are in the area of inventing new medical concerns): *geriatric* medicine is an expanding speciality and *gerontology* a growing study. Qualified persons are paid at appropriate rates to be professors of it. We are therefore well advanced in the production of another army of professionals, researchers and specialised carers who live off the 'geriatric burden' and, of course, add to its cost.

During one or two of the addresses given to the conference, and in a good deal of discussions, I had an uncomfortable sense of a consensus between the parties interested in ageing that we should all be organised to be generally caring and professionally colluding so that we interested parties could do good acceptably and be paid for it.

For my own professional and priestly reasons I was partly amused and partly inclined to be annoyed by the gracious way that one or two of the medics addressing the conference confessed how they had discovered that – regardless of basic questions of belief – clergy could be quite useful members of 'therapeutic teams'. There was no serious consideration of faith as relating to human reality, human potential and the possibility of divine or transcendent resources (God perhaps?) open to human beings. Everything was reduced to a question of 'spirituality', which I am increasingly finding to be a weasel word used to obfuscate or avoid basic questions of reality.

'Spirituality' has become a substitute for 'faith' and is rapidly shrunk to be, in effect, 'religiosity', something to be indulged in according to personal and individual taste. For example, one presentation included the confident judgement that, with respect to the therapeutic effect, the important thing in matters of spirituality was religious *certainty,* whatever one was certain about. Such statements betray no concern for engagement in life and death from beginning to end, or the extent to which religious certainties can either open people up to wider realities or close them down. Therapy was the be-all and end-all, while reality and commitment seemed to stretch no further.

Such boxing up of religion is perhaps understandable. After all, when one is living with (as well as living on) medical, social and financial problems of caring for the aged there is little spare time or energy to pursue matters of truth or to explore the deeper realities that assist us to face death, such as the demands and offers of love.

As the conference went on I became increasingly troubled about the financial and economic implications of all this talk about caring, research into geriatrics and multiplication of specialists providing specialist therapies. Where was the money to come from? There are tough questions here at the very basic level of financing supply and demand and the politics connected to all this, both in particular institutions and at national level.

I was reminded of an international gathering I attended once, arranged by the Christian Medical Commission of the World Council of Churches. During one presentation it suddenly struck me that the medical services and equipment being outlined by one Scandinavian team as the response to a health problem in a particular third world country would actually require teams in double figures to supply it to each individual. This in a case where the national budget could not stretch to more than a few clinics for overall health care.

This development of specialisms and the focus on the professional organisation of dying reminded me of another occasion round about 1968, when I attended the first National American Conference on Thanatology. (More Greek for specialisms! *Thanatos* is Greek for death.) Then I was moved to remark to the conference that we had all come to a pretty pass in our human living. Not only did we need manuals on sexuality in order that we should make love correctly, but we now found the need for a nationwide organisation to advise us on dying. Have we lost any shared and simple grasp on living and loving, hoping and helping during our common human experience of dying?

More than 30 years on, sitting in another conference, while both speakers and participants exchanged evidence of some remarkable caring and intelligent organisation, everyone still seemed immersed in their own approaches, their own needs and their own funding. But to do so is to inhabit an unreal world financially, economically and politically that limits our shared human scope to live and cope realistically.

At the time of my acceptance of the invitation I did not know the details of the programme for the five days of the conference, so the suggested title of my address to the closing session, 'Geriatric Burden or Elderly Blessing?', was offered on a hunch, but in the event I believe it has proved apt. The specialised and compartmentalised concerns displayed in the keynote speeches presented examples of the reduction of *vital* and *communal* areas of human living and dying, to problems, practices, professions and funding. This is in danger of reducing everything to do with growing old to problems rather than seeking the insights and practices to promote the universal human experiences of ageing to be about *people*.

The present social trend is to make the 'ageing' a constituency, a problem, a profession and even a business (every activity reported was accompanied by the perpetual quest for necessary funding). All this emphasis on the burdens involved means that no one is concentrating on the resources which the ageing surely either do represent or must be stimulated and invited to represent. It is all geriatric burden with no evident concern about evoking and making use of elderly blessing.

While composing these further reflections I have come to wonder what effect it might have had on our common awareness, and our deliberations, if the conference had been entitled say: 'Getting Old, Making the Most of it and Managing', or even: 'Getting Old, Getting Help and Getting By' – that might at least have helped to concentrate the minds and spirits of all concerned on the ageing as people, neighbours, fellow human beings and fellow citizens and so fellow *resources*.

'Getting help and getting by' is not a bad synonym for what 'spirituality' ought to be and how it may serve if properly translated into a pilgrimage into the realities of life in relation to the realities of one another and to God; that is to say, as encounters with fundamental realities and not expressions of and explorations into therapy.

Of course, this 'bewilderment of therapies' cannot merely be blamed on the practitioners and innovators and pioneers. It is what modern oldies have come to expect. We are as much influenced by the technical, transactional and individualised practices and expectations of our market-driven, greed-oriented and individual consumption-directed society as our younger neighbours. There is plenty of complaint about 'being robbed of our pensions', for there is no more understanding among the oldies than among the middle-aged and younger that a money figure as a financial entitlement is worth only whatever that money figure can purchase at the time it comes to be cashed. Likewise many middle-class oldies feel an absolute entitlement to a continuing retirement of travels and holidays regardless of where we all are economically.

Again, most people seem to regard any suggestion of raising the pension age as a gross exploitation and deprivation. Yet, as part of society, why should we not have to work longer if modern advances mean that we are fit to do so and social productivity requires it?

Take the political and economic issues of petrol consumption and transport. Oldies, as much as middle-aged, middle-class parents and the young, have the citizenly responsibility to encourage the appropriate authorities to provide decent bus services if we are to escape gridlock, overwhelming pollution and unsustainable over-dependence on petrol.

Considerations such as these point to the conclusion that unless older citizens, middle-aged citizens, tax-payers in general and the young find a way to live in communities with neighbourly care and develop disciplined ways of consumption, limitation and taxation, society as a whole will suffer. What future do we face if everyone shrinks into their interest groups, professional struggles or single issues? Society will become ever more stressed, more combative and divisive. In such conditions the truly weak and helpless aged, as with the rest of the chronically sick and hopelessly poor, can only be condemned to miserable housing, inadequate care and a general sense of hopelessness.

One of the central issues for us all, regardless of age, profession, classification, health or wealth, is how to find – or to be found by – the realism and faith to live co-operatively. We cannot find solutions in the endless multiplication of specialist treatment centres and the growth of individualised therapies and spiritualities for which funds have to be generally raised. The only feasible way forward is for everyone, of whatever age or classification, to learn how to work together to contribute what they can as long as they can to keeping societies and neighbours going. Then there may be enough productive people around to be taxed or tithed to pay enough to provide reasonable and sustainable care to all who truly cannot help themselves.

I do not intend any of these remarks to be an attack on either the motives or the achievements of the practitioners, explorers and carers who took part in the conference. But I am pretty clear that in the field of ageing and living hopefully – as in all the other problem areas of our current society – we are reaching the limits of mere multiplication and funding. Those of us who are committed to making positive responses to the problems, possibilities and promises of living and working together in this vast human field of getting old, getting on and getting by have to be conscious of the wider dimensions and demands of our concerns and experiences.

It is unproductive to focus organisation and provision on the problematic elderly alone. Everyone – including of course the elderly ourselves – has to find appropriate ways of developing as neighbourly citizens and political neighbours who are out to change our ways of living together for the better of all.

Only *society* together and *communities* together, drawing on all the resources of the able bodied and the less able bodied, can face up hopefully and realistically to the challenge of an ageing society. We can do so by discovering and encouraging the positive wisdoms and resources of those growing older. Unless we discover our elderly blessing capacity we shall be less and less able to positively bear our burdens – and even worse, we ignore some blessings in them also.

References

Achenberg, W. A. (1985) 'Religion in the lives of the elderly.' In G. Lesnoff-Caravalglia (ed) *Values, Ethics and Aging.* New York: Human Science Press.

Adams, N. (1995) 'Spirituality, science and therapy.' *Australian and New Zealand Journal of Family Therapy 16,* 4, 201–208.

Ahrendt, H. (1958) *The Human Condition.* Chicago: University of Chicago Press.

Airey, J., Hammond, G., Kent, P. and Moffitt, L. (2002) *Frequently Asked Questions on Spirituality and Religion.* Derby: CCOA.

Albom, M. (1997) *Tuesdays with Morrie.* New York: Doubleday.

Allen, B. (ed) (2002) *Religious Practice and People with Dementia.* Newcastle: CCOA Dementia Project.

Annells, M. (1996) 'Grounded theory method: philosophical perspectives, paradigm of inquiry, and postmodernism.' *Qualitative Health Research 6,* 3.

Anson, O., Antonovsky, A. and Sagy, S. (1990) 'Religiosity and well-being among retirees: a question of causality.' *Behaviour, Health and Aging 1,* 85–87.

Antonovsky, A. (1987) *Unravelling the Mystery of Health: How People Manage Stress and Stay Well.* San Francisco: Jossey-Bass.

Armatowski, J. (2001) 'Attitudes towards death and dying among persons in the fourth quarter of life.' In D. O. Moberg (ed) *Aging and Spirituality.* New York: Haworth Pastoral Press.

Ball, R. A. and Goodyear, R. K. (1991) 'Self-reported professional practices of Christian psychotherapists.' *Journal of Psychology and Christianity 10,* 144–153.

Baltes, P. B. and Baltes, M. M. (eds) (1990) *Successful Aging: Perspectives from the Behavioral Sciences.* New York: Cambridge University Press.

Battista, J. and Almond, R. (1973) 'The development of meaning in life.' *Psychiatry 36,* 409–427.

Bellah, R. N., Madsen, R., Sullivan, W. M., Swidler, A. and Tipton, S. M. (1985) *Habits of the Heart: Individualism and Commitment to American Life.* Berkeley: University of California Press.

Bender, M. (2002) 'Do charities have to devalue their clients to get donations?' *Journal of Dementia Care 10,* 4.

Bergin, A. E. (1991) 'Values and religious issues in psychotherapy and mental health.' *American Psychologist 46*, 394–403.

Bergin, A. E. and Payne, I. R. (1993) 'Self-reported professional practices of Christian psychotherapists.' In E. L. Worthington Jr (ed) *Psychotherapy and Religious Values.* Grand Rapids, MI: Baker.

Bhagavad Gita (1905) Trans. by A. Besant and B. Das. London and Benares: Theological Publishing Society.

Bianchi, E. (1984) *Aging as a Spiritual Journey.* New York: Crossroad Publishing.

Blanchard-Fields, F. and Norris, L. (1995) 'The development of wisdom.' In M. A. Kimble, S. H. McFadden, J. W. Ellor and J. J. Seeber (eds) *Aging, Spirituality and Religion: A Handbook.* Minneapolis: Augsburg Fortress Press.

Bleathman, C. and Morton, I. (1991) 'Validation therapy: extracts from 20 groups with dementia sufferers.' *Journal of Advanced Nursing 17*, 658–666.

Boden, C. (1998) *Who Will I Be When I Die?* San Francisco: HarperCollins.

Borg, M. J. (1998) *The God We Never Knew: Beyond Dogmatic Religion to a More Authentic Contemporary Faith.* San Francisco: HarperCollins.

Bromiley, G. W. (ed) (1985) *Theological Dictionary of the New Testament.* Grand Rapids, MI: Eerdmans.

Brough, B. S. (1998) *Alzheimer's With Love.* Lismore, NSW: Southern Cross University Press.

Bultmann, R. (1963) Page 138 footnote in J. A. T. Robinson and D. Edwards (eds) *The Honest To God Debate.* London: SCM Press.

Byrd, R. C. (1988) 'Positive therapeutic effects of intercessory prayer in a coronary care unit population.' *Southern Medical Journal 81*, 7, 826–829.

Cable, S. (2000) 'Clinical experience: preparation of medical and nursing students for collaborative practices.' Unpublished PhD dissertation, University of Dundee.

Cairns, R. (2001) 'Spirituality and mental health.' Paper presented at the Mental Health and Spirituality in Later Life: Creative Approaches to Communication and Care Conference, Canberra, September.

Canda, E. (1995) 'Existential family therapy: using the concepts of Victor Frankl.' *Journal of Contemporary Human Services 76*, 451–452.

Carlson, R. and Shield, B. (1989) *Healers on Healing.* Los Angeles: Tarchet.

Carroll, L. P. and Dyckman, K. M. (1986) *Chaos or Creation: Spirituality in Mid-life.* New York: Paulist Press.

Chekola, M. G. (1975) 'The concept of happiness.' University of Michigan doctoral dissertation. *Dissertation Abstracts International 35*, 4609A.

Cobb, M. and Robshaw, V. (1998) *The Spiritual Challenge of Health Care.* Edinburgh: Churchill Livingstone.

Cohen, G. D. (1988) *The Brain in Human Aging.* New York: Springer.

Coleman, P. G. (1992) 'Questioning of religious meanings in later life.' *British Psychological Society Special Interest Group in the Elderly Newsletter 42*, 23–26.

Coleman, P. G. (1993) 'Adjustment in later life.' In J. Bond, P. G. Coleman and S. M. Peace (eds) *Ageing in Society: An Introduction to Social Gerontology*, 2nd edn. London: Sage.

Coleman, P. G. and McCulloch, A. (1990) 'Societal change, values and social support: exploratory studies into adjustment in late life.' *Journal of Aging Studies 4*, 321–332.

Coleman, P. G., McKiernan, F., Mills, M. A. and Speck, P. (2002) 'Spiritual belief and quality of life: the experience of older bereaved spouses.' *Quality in Ageing – Policy, Practice and Research 3*, 20–26.

Courtenay, B. C., Poon, L. W., Martin, P. and Clayton, G. M. (1992) 'Religiosity and adaptation in oldest-old.' *International Journal of Aging and Human Development 34*, 47–64.

Craig, C. (2001) *Celebrating the Person: A Practical Approach to Art Activities*. Stirling: University of Stirling Dementia Services Development Centre.

Crisp, J. and Taylor, C. (2001) Australian adaptation of Potter and Perry's *Fundamentals of Nursing*. Marrickville: Mosby.

Cross, F. (ed) (1997) *The Oxford Dictionary of the Christian Church*, 3rd edn. Oxford: Oxford University Press.

Crumbaugh, J. C. and Maholick, L. T. (1969) *Manual of Instructions for the Purpose in Life Test*. Brookport, IL: Psychometric Affiliates.

Culberson, C. E. (1977) 'A holistic view of joy in relation to psychotherapy derived from Lowen, Maslow, and Assagoli.' Doctoral dissertation. *Dissertation Abstracts International 38*, 2853B.

Culliford, L. (2002) 'Spiritual care and psychiatric treatment: an introduction.' *Advances in Psychiatric Treatment 8*, 249–261.

Culligan, K. (1996) *Spirituality and Healing in Medicine*. New York: American Press.

Cumming, E. and Henry, W. E. (1961) *Growing Old: The Process of Disengagement*. New York: Basic Books.

Davenport, E. (2000) 'Clinical guidelines and the translation of texts into care: overcoming professional conflicts concerning evidence based practice.' *Journal of Documentation 56*, 5, 505–519.

Decker, L. R. (1993) 'The role of trauma in spiritual development. Special issue: trauma and transcendence.' *Journal of Humanistic Psychology 33*, 33–46.

Dementia in Scotland Newsletter (2002) *38*, 1.

Dennis, D. (1995) 'Humanistic neuroscience, mentality and spirituality.' *Journal of Humanistic Psychology 35*, 34–72.

De Rogario, L. (1997) 'Spirituality in the lives of people with disability and chronic illness: a creative paradigm of wholeness and reconstitution.' *Disability and Rehabilitation: An International Multidisciplinary Journal 19*, 423–427.

Diener, E. (1984) 'Subjective well-being.' *Psychological Bulletin 95*, 542–575.

Diener, E., Suh, M. E., Lucas, E. R. and Smith, L. H. (1999) 'Subjective well-being: three decades of progress.' *Psychological Bulletin 125*, 276–302.

Donahue, M. J. (1985) 'Intrinsic and extrinsic religiousness: review and meta-analysis.' *Journal of Personality and Social Psychology 48*, 400–419.

Eliade, M. (1965) *The Myth of the Eternal Return.* New York: Pantheon Books.

Ellison, C. G. (1993) 'Religious involvement and self perception among Americans.' *Social Forces 71*, 1027–1055.

Ellison, C. G., Gey, D. A. and Glass, T. (1991) 'Does religious commitment contribute to individual life satisfaction?' *Social Forces 68*, 100–123.

Erikson, E. H. (1963) *Childhood and Society*, 2nd edn. New York: Norton.

Erikson, E. H. and Erikson, J. M. (1997) *The Life Cycle Completed.* New York: Norton.

Erikson, E. H., Erikson, J. M. and Kivnick, H. Q. (1986) *Vital Involvement in Old Age.* New York: Norton.

Everett, D. (1996) *Forget Me Not: The Spiritual Care of People with Alzheimer's Disease.* Edmonton: Inkwell Press.

Fabella, V., Lee, P. K. H. and Suh, D. K. (eds) (1992) *Asian Christian Spirituality: Reclaiming Traditions.* Maryknoll, NY: Orbis Books.

Farrer, A. (1960) *Said or Sung.* London: Faith Press.

Fischer, K. R. (1998) *Winter Grace: Spirituality and Aging.* Nashville: Upper Room Books.

Fowler, J. W. (1981) *Stages of Faith: The Psychology of Human Development and the Quest for Meaning.* New York: Harper and Row.

Frankl, V. E. (1967) 'What is a man?' *Kaleidoscope,* September, 151.

Frankl, V. E. (1969) *The Doctor and the Soul.* New York: Bantam.

Frankl, V. E. (1978) *The Unheard Cry for Meaning.* New York: Simon and Schuster.

Frankl, V. E. (1984) *Man's Search for Meaning.* New York: Washington Square Press.

Froggatt, A. and Moffitt, L. (1997) 'Spiritual needs and religious practice in dementia care.' In M. Marshall (ed) *State of the Art in Dementia Care.* London: Centre for Policy on Ageing.

Gadow, S. and Berg, G. (1978) 'Towards more human meanings of ageing: ideals and images from philosophy and art.' In S. F. Spicker (ed) *Aging and the Elderly: Humanistic Perspectives in Gerontology.* Atlantic Island, NJ: Humanities Press.

Gallup, G. (1982) *The Gallup Poll.* New York: Random House.

Gallup, G. (1988) *The Gallup Poll.* New York: Random House.

Gallup, G. Jr. and Castelli, J. (1989) *The People's Religion: American Faith in the 90s.* New York: Macmillan.

Ganje-Fling, M. A. and McCarthy, P. (1996) 'Impact of childhood social abuse on client spiritual development: counselling implications.' *Journal of Counselling and Development 74*, 253–258.

George, L. K. (1988) 'Social participation in later life: black–white differences.' In J. S. Jackson (ed) *The Black American Elderly: Research on Physical and Psychosocial Health.* New York: Springer.

Gibson, F. (1998) 'Unmasking dementia.' *Community Care* supplement, 'Inside Dementia', 29 Oct–4 Nov.

Gibson, F. (1999) 'Can we risk person-centred communication?' *Journal of Dementia Care 7*, 5, 20–24.

Glaser, B. G. (1978) *Theoretical Sensitivity.* Mill Valley, CA: Sociology Press.

Glaser, B. G. and Strauss, A. L. (1967) *The Discovery of Grounded Theology.* Chicago: Aldine Atherton.

Goldsmith, M. (1996) *Hearing the Voice of People with Dementia.* London: Jessica Kingsley Publishers.

Goodenough, U. (1998) *The Sacred Depths of Nature.* Oxford: Oxford University Press.

Gopaul-McNicol, S.-A. (1997) 'The role of religion in psychotherapy: a cross-cultural examination.' *Journal of Contemporary Psychotherapy 27*, 37–48.

Graber, D. and Johnson, J. (2001) 'Spirituality and health care organisations.' *Journal of Health Care Management 46*, 39–52.

Greenhalgh, T. (2002) 'Intuition and evidence – uneasy bedfellows.' *British Journal of General Practice 52*, 478, 395–399.

Hadway, C. K. (1978) 'Life satisfaction and religion: a re-analysis.' *Social Forces 57*, 636–647.

Hall, M. E. L. and Hall, T. W. (1997) 'Integration in the therapy room: an overview of the literature.' *Journal of Psychology and Theology 25*, 1, 129–134.

Hall, T. A. (1995) 'Spiritual effects of childhood sexual abuse in adult Christian women.' *Journal of Psychology and Theology 23*, 2, 129–134.

Hammond, G. and Moffitt, L. (2000) *Spiritual Care: Guidelines for Care Plans.* Newcastle: CCOA Dementia Project.

Hanlon, P., Gilhooly, M. and White, B. (2002) *PREVAIL: The Paisley Renfrew Evaluation of Vitality and Ageing in Later Life. Determinants of Good Health and Successful Ageing. A Detailed Examination of the Healthiest Surviving Members of the Midspan Cohort.* Final Report on Grant Number K/PR/E/2/D372. Edinburgh: Chief Scientist Office, Scottish Executive.

Hare Duke, M. (2001) *One Foot in Heaven: Growing Older and Living to the Full.* London: Triangle/SPCK.

Harris, D. K. (1990) *Sociology of Aging.* New York: Harper and Row.

Harris, M. (1991) *Dance of the Spirit: The Seven Steps of Women's Spirituality.* New York and London: Bantam.

Harrold, C. F. (1943) *A Newman Treasury.* London: Longmans, Green and Co.

Hassan, R. (1995) *Suicide Explained: The Australian Experience.* Melbourne: Melbourne University Press.

Hay, D. and Hunt, K. (2000) *The Spirituality of People Who Don't Go to Church.* Final Report. Nottingham: Adult Spirituality Project, Nottingham University.

Hebb, D. O. (1978) 'On watching myself get old.' *Psychology Today 23,* 31–33.

Heelas, P. (ed) (1998) *Religion, Modernity and Postmodernity.* Oxford: Blackwell.

Heinz, D. (1994) 'Finishing the story: aging, spirituality and the work of culture.' *Journal of Religious Gerontology 9,* 1, 3–19.

Helminiak, D. A. (1996) 'A scientific spirituality: the interface of psychology and theology.' *International Journal for the Psychology of Religion 86,* 1–19.

Hobbs, N. (1962) 'Sources of gain in psychotherapy.' *American Psychologist 17,* 742–748.

Hood, R. W. Jr., Spilka, B., Hunsberger, B. and Gorsuch, R. (1996) *The Psychology of Religion: An Empirical Approach,* 2nd edn. New York: Guilford Press.

Howse, K. (1999) *Religion, Spirituality and Older People.* London: Centre for Policy on Ageing.

Hudson, R. (2000) 'The economic burden of aged care: some theological reflections.' *St Mark's Review 181,* 16–23.

Hudson, R. (2003) 'The spirit of the age and the spirit of ageing.' *Sacred Space 4,* 1, 5–11.

Hunt, L. (1997) 'The past in the present: an introduction to trauma re-emerging in old age.' In L. Hunt, M. Marshall and C. Rowlings (eds) *Past Trauma in Late Life.* London: Jessica Kingsley Publishers.

Ignatieff, M. (1984) *The Needs of Strangers.* London: Chatto and Windus/Hogarth Press.

Ishii-Kuntz, M. and Lee, G. R. (1987) 'Status of the elderly: an extension of the theory.' *Journal of Marriage and the Family 49,* 413–420.

Jahoda, M. (1958) *Current Concepts of Positive Mental Health.* New York: Basic Books.

Jantzen, G. M. (1998) *Becoming Divine: Towards a Feminist Philosophy of Religion.* Manchester: Manchester University Press.

Jenkins, R. A. and Pargament, K. I. (1995) 'Religion and spirituality as a resource for coping with cancer.' *Journal of Psychosocial Oncology 13,* 51–74.

Jenny, S. and Oropeza, M. (1993) *Memories in the Making: A Programme of Creative Art Expressions for Alzheimer's Patients.* Orange County, CA: Alzheimer's Association.

Jenson, R. W. (1997a) *Systematic Theology: The Triune God.* Oxford: Oxford University Press.

Jenson, R. W. (1997b) *Systematic Theology: The Works of God*. Oxford: Oxford University Press.

Jewell, A. (ed) (1999) *Spirituality and Ageing*. London: Jessica Kingsley Publishers.

Jungel, E. (1976) *The Doctrine of the Trinity: God's Being is in Becoming*. Edinburgh: Scottish Academic Press. Trans. by Horton Harris of *Gottes Sein ist in Werden* (1966). Tubingen: J. C. B. Mohr.

Kaldor, P. (1987) *Who Goes Where? Who Doesn't Care?* Homebush West: Lancer Books.

Kalish, R. A. and Reynolds, D. K. (1976) *Death and Ethnicity: A Psychocultural Study*. Los Angeles: University of Southern California Press.

Kane, D., Cheston, S. and Green, J. (1993) 'Perceptions of God by survivors of childhood sexual abuse: an exploratory study in an underresearched area.' *Journal of Psychology and Theology 21*, 3, 228–237.

Keen, S. (1994) *Hymns to an Unknown God*. New York: Bantam.

Kennedy, J. E. and Kanthamani, H. (1995) 'An explorative study of effects of paranormal and spiritual experiences on peoples' lives and well-being.' *Journal of the American Society for Psychical Research 89*, 249–264.

Kennedy, J. E., Kanthamani, H. and Palmer, K. (1994) 'Psychic and spiritual experiences, health, well-being, and meaning in life.' *Journal of Parapsychology 58*, 353–383.

Killick, J. (1999) 'Pathways through pain.' *Journal of Dementia Care 7*, 22–24.

Killick, J. and Cordonnier, C. (2001) *Openings: Dementia Poems and Photographs*. London: Hawker.

Kimble, M. (2000) 'Aging in the Christian tradition.' In T. Cole, R. Kastenbaum and R. Ray (eds) *Handbook of the Humanities and Aging*, 2nd edn. New York: Springer.

Kimble, M. (2002) 'Beyond the biomedical paradigm: generating a spiritual vision of aging.' In MacKinlay, E. B., Ellor, J. and Pickard. (eds) *Aging, Spirituality and Pastoral Care*. New York: Haworth.

Kimble, M., McFadden, S. H., Ellor, J. W. and Seeber, J. J. (eds) (1995) *Aging, Spirituality, and Religion: A Handbook*. Minneapolis: Augsburg Fortress Press.

King, M., Speck, P. and Thomas, A. (1995) 'The Royal Free interview for religious and spiritual beliefs: development and standardization.' *Psychological Medicine 25*, 1125–1134.

King, M., Speck, P. and Thomas, A. (2001) 'The Royal Free interview for spiritual and religious beliefs: development and validation of a self-report version.' *Psychological Medicine 31*, 1015–1023.

King, U. (1993) *Women and Spirituality: Voices of Protest and Promise*. London: Macmillan.

King, U. (1996) *Spirit of Fire: The Life and Vision of Teilhard de Chardin*. New York: Orbis Books.

King, U. (1999) 'Spirituality, ageing and gender.' In A. Jewell (ed) *Spirituality and Ageing*. London: Jessica Kingsley Publishers.

Kitwood, T. (1997) *Dementia Reconsidered*. Buckingham: Open University Press.

Kivley, L. R. (1986) 'Therapist attitude toward including religious issues in therapy.' *Journal of Psychology and Christianity 5*, 37–45.

Koenig, H. G. (1994) *Aging and God: Spiritual Pathways to Mental Health in Midlife and Later Years*. New York: Haworth Pastoral Press.

Koenig, H. G. (1995) *Research on Religion and Ageing: An Annotated Bibliography*. Westport, CT: Greenwood Press.

Krippner, S. and Welch, P. (1992) *Spiritual Dimensions of Healing*. New York: Irvington.

Kubler-Ross, E. (1975) *Death: The Final Stage of Growth*. New York: Simon and Schuster.

Lamb, W. and Thomson, H. (2001) 'Wholeness, dignity and the aging self: a conversation between philosophy and theology.' In E. MacKinlay, J. Ellor and S. Pickard (eds) *Aging, Spirituality and Pastoral Care: A Multi-national Perspective*. New York: Haworth Pastoral Press.

Larson, D., Theilman, S. B., Greenwold, M. A., Lyons, J. S., Post, S. G., Sherrill, K. A., Wood, G. G. and Larson, S. S. (1993) 'Religious content in the DSM-III-R Glossary of Technical Terms.' *American Journal of Psychiatry 150*, 12, 1884–1885.

Lewis, A. E. (2001) *Between Cross and Resurrection: A Theology of Holy Saturday*. Grand Rapids, MI: Eerdmans.

Lindgren, K. N. and Coursey, R. D. (1995) 'Spirituality and serious mental illness: a two part study.' *Psychosocial Rehabilitation Journal 18*, 3, 93–111.

Lloyd, M. (2003) 'Challenging Depression: Taking a Spiritually Enhanced Approach.' (Article submitted for publication).

Long, J. D., Anderson, J. and Williams, R. L. (1990) 'Life reflection by older kinsmen about critical life issues.' *Educational Gerontology 16*, 61–71.

Lopez, O. L., Becker, J. T., Wisniewski, S., Saxton, J., Kaufer, D. I. and Dekosky, S. T. (2002) 'Cholinesterase inhibitor treatment alters the natural history of Alzheimer's disease.' *Journal of Neurology, Neurosurgery and Psychiatry 72*, 3, 310–314.

Loyola, I. (1973) *The Spiritual Exercises of Saint Ignatius Loyola*. Trans. T. Corbishley. Wheathampstead: Anthony Clarke.

Luke, H. (1997) *Old Age: Journey into Simplicity*. New York: Parabola Books.

MacKinlay, E. B. (1998) 'The spiritual dimension of ageing: meaning in life, response to meaning and well being in ageing.' Unpublished doctoral dissertation. Melbourne: La Trobe University.

MacKinlay, E. B. (2001a) *The Spiritual Dimension of Ageing*. London: Jessica Kingsley Publishers.

MacKinlay, E. B. (2001b) 'Understanding the ageing process: a developmental perspective of the psychological and spiritual dimensions.' *Journal of Religious Gerontology 12*, 3/4, 111–112.

MacKinlay, E. B. (2001c) 'Health, healing and wholeness in frail elderly people.' *Journal of Religious Gerontology 13*, 2, 25–34.

MacKinlay, E. B., Trevitt, C. and Coady, M. (2002–4) 'Finding meaning in the experience of dementia: the place of spiritual reminiscence work.' Project awarded Australian Research Council Linkage Grant (2002–2004) to fund research through one or more universities with industry partners.

MacKinlay, E. B., Trevitt, C. and Hobart, S. (2002) 'The search for meaning: quality of life for the person with dementia.' University of Canberra Collaborative Grant 2001. Unpublished Project Report, February.

Macquarrie, J. (1982) *In Search of Humanity.* London: SCM Press.

McNamara, L. (2001) 'Ethics and ageing in the 21st century.' *Journal of Religious Gerontology 12*, 3–4, 5–30.

McFadden, S. (1995) 'Religion and well-being in aging persons in an aging society.' *Journal of Social Issues 51*, 161–175.

McKinlay, A. (1998) *Inner ≥ Out: A Journey With Dementia.* Rothsay: Charcoal Press.

McSherry, W. (2001) 'Spiritual crisis? Call a nurse.' In H. Orchard (ed) *Spirituality in Health Care Contexts.* London: Jessica Kingsley Publishers.

Maddi, S. (1967) 'The existential neurosis.' *Journal of Abnormal Psychology 72*, 311–325.

Mahoney, J. M. and Graci, M. G. (1999) 'The meaning and correlates of spirituality.' *Death Studies 23*, 521–528.

Maton, K. I. (1989) 'The stress-buffering role of spiritual support: cross-sectional and prospective investigations.' *Journal for the Scientific Study of Religion 28*, 310–323.

Merton, T. (1972) *Seeds of Contemplation.* Wheathampstead: Anthony Clarke.

Miller, B. (2000) 'Functional correlates of musical and visual ability in frontotemporal dementia.' *British Journal of Psychiatry 176*, 458–463.

Miller, F. (1998) *The Trial of Faith of Saint Thérèse of Lisieux.* New York: Alba House.

Miller, J. (1990) 'Goodbye to all this.' *Independent on Sunday* (Sunday Review section), 15 April.

Moberg, D. O. (1990) 'Spiritual maturity and wholeness in later years.' *Journal of Religious Gerontology 7*, 1–2, 5–24.

Moberg, D. O. (ed) (2001) *Aging and Spirituality.* New York: Haworth Pastoral Press.

Mohan, K. (2001) 'Spirituality and well-being: an overview.' In C. Matthijs (ed) *Integral Psychology.* Pondicherry: Sri Aurbindo Ashram Press.

Moody, H. R. (1992) *Ethics in and Aging Society.* Baltimore: Johns Hopkins University Press.

Mookherjee, H. N. (1994) 'Effects of religiosity and selected variables on the perception of well-being.' *Journal of Social Psychology 134*, 403–405.

Moran, P. (1990) 'Children as victims of sexual abuse.' In S. Rossetti (ed) *Slayer of the Soul.* Mystic, CT: Twenty-third Publications.

Mullan, M. and Killick, J. (2001) *Responding to Music.* Stirling: Dementia Services Development Centre, University of Stirling.

Musurillo, H. (1961) *From Glory to Glory: Texts from Gregory of Nyssa's Mystical Writings.* London: Darton, Longman and Todd.

Myers, D. G. and Diener, E. (eds) (1995) 'Who is happy?' *Psychological Science 6*, 10–19.

Neame, A. (1997) *The Little Way: The Spirituality of Thérèse of Lisieux.* London: Darton, Longman and Todd. Translation of *La Gloire et le Mendiant* by Bernard Bro. Paris: Les Editions du Cerf.

Neil, A. (1995) 'Spirituality, science and therapy.' *Australian and New Zealand Journal of Family Therapy 16*, 201–208.

Neuhaus, R. (2001) 'September 11 – before and after.' *First Things (Journal of Religion and Public Life) 117*, 65–84.

Newman, J. H. (1893) *Meditations on Christian Doctrine.* Quoted in C. F. Harrold (1943) *A Newman Treasury.* London: Longmans, Green and Co.

Nichol, D. (1998) *The Testing of Hearts: A Pilgrim's Journey.* London: Darton, Longman and Todd.

Nouwen, H. J. M. (1994) *The Return of the Prodigal Son.* London: Darton, Longman and Todd.

Nouwen, H. J. M. and Gaffney, W. J. (1976) *Ageing: The Fulfillment of Life.* Garden City, NY: Image Books.

Nusberg, C. (1983) 'Filial responsibility still required in Hungary.' *Aging International 9*, 7–9.

Orchard, H. (ed) (2001) *Spirituality in Health Care Contexts.* London: Jessica Kingsley Publishers.

Ornish, D. (1990) *Dr. Dean Ornish's Programme for Reversing Heart Disease.* New York: Random House.

Paloutzian, R. F. (1996) *Invitation to the Psychology of Religion*, 2nd edn. Needham Heights, MA: Allyn and Bacon.

Pargament, K. I. (1996) 'Religious methods of coping: resources for the conservation and transformation of significance.' In E. P. Shafranske (ed) *Religion and Clinical Practice of Psychology.* Washington, DC: American Psychological Association.

Pargament, K. I., Echemendia, R. J., Johnson, S., Cook, P., McGath, C., Myers, J. and Brannick, M. (1987) 'The conservative church: psychosocial advantages and disadvantages.' *American Journal of Community Psychology 15*, 269–286.

Patricia, L. R. (1998) 'Spirituality among adult survivors of childhood violence: a literature review.' *Journal of Transpersonal Psychology 30*, 39–51.

Payne, I. R., Bergin, A. E., Biclema, K. A. and Jenkins, P. H. (1991) 'Review of religion and mental health: prevention and the enhancement of psychological functioning.' *Prevention in Human Services 9*, 11–40.

Peck, S. (1990) *The Different Drum.* London: Arrow.

Pitskhelauri, G. Z. (1982) *The Long-living of Soviet Georgia.* New York: Human Sciences Press.

Post, S. (1992) 'DSM-III-R and religion.' *Social Science and Medicine 25*, 1, 81–90.

Post, S. (1994) *The Moral Challenge of Alzheimer's.* Baltimore: Johns Hopkins University Press.

Potter, D. (1994) *Seeing the Blossom.* London: Faber and Faber.

Princeton Religious Research Center (1994) 'Importance of religion climbing again.' *Emerging Trends 16*, 1–4.

Pullman, P. (2000) *His Dark Materials.* London: Scholastic Children's Books.

Quoist, M. (1963) *Prayers of Life.* London: Gill and Macmillan.

Rahner, K. (1990) In P. Imhof and H. Biallowons (eds) *Faith in a Wintry Season: Conversations and Interviews with Karl Rahner in the Last Years of His Life.* Trans. H. D. Egan. New York: Crossroad.

Reese, H. W. (1997) 'Spirituality, belief, and action.' *Journal of Mind and Behaviour 18*, 29–51.

Reid, H. (2002) *Outside Verdict: An Old Kirk in a New Scotland.* Edinburgh: Saint Andrew Press.

Reker, G. T. and Wong, P. T. P. (1988) 'Aging as an individual process: toward a theory of personal meaning.' In J. E. Birren and V. L. Bengtson (eds) *Emergent Theories of Aging.* New York: Springer.

Rilke, R. M. (1963) *Letters to a Young Poet.* New York: Norton.

Robson, C. (2002) *Real World Research: A Resource for Social Scientists and Practitioner-researchers.* Oxford: Blackwell.

Rosel, N. (1988) 'Clarification and application of Erik Erikson's eighth stage of man.' *International Journal of Aging and Human Development 27*, 11–23.

Ross, J. L. (1994) 'Working with patients within their religious contexts: religion, spirituality and the secular therapist.' *Journal of Systematic Therapies 13*, 7–15.

Rowe, J. W. and Kahn, R. L. (1997) 'Successful ageing.' *The Gerontologist 37*, 4, 433–440.

Ryan, D. (2003) 'Spirituality: integrating self, system and environment in contemporary Scottish Health Care?' Paper given to conference on Spirituality in Contemporary Scotland, Glasgow University, 21–22 February.

Sappington, A. A. (1994) 'Psychology for the practice of the presence of God: putting psychology at the service of the Church.' *Journal of Psychology and Christianity 13*, 5–16.

Sargent, N. M. (1989) 'Spirituality and adult survivors of child sexual abuse: some treatment issues.' In S. M. Sgroi (ed) *Vulnerable Populations: Sexual Abuse Treatment for Children, Adult Survivors, Offenders and Persons with Mental Retardation*, vol. 2. Lexington, MA: D. C. Heath.

Schafen, W. E. and King, M. (1990) 'Religiousness and stress among college students: a survey report.' *Journal of College Student Development 31*, 336–341.

Scheier, M. P. and Carver, C. S. (1987) 'Dispositional optimism and physical well-being: the influence of generalized outcome expectancies on health.' *Journal of Personality 55*, 169–210.

Schick, F. L. (ed) (1986) *Statistical Handbook on Aging Americans*. Phoenix, AZ: Oryx Press.

Schultz-Hipp, P. L. (2001) 'Do spirituality and religiosity increase with age?' In D. O. Moberg (ed) *Ageing and Spirituality*. New York: Haworth Pastoral Press.

Seeber, J. (1990) 'Spiritual maturity and wholeness – a concept whose time has come.' In J. Seeber (ed) *Spiritual Maturity in Later Years*. New York: Haworth Pastoral Press.

Seedhouse, D. (1995) '"Well-being": health promotions red herring.' *Health Promotion International 10*, 61–67.

Seligman, M. E. P. (1991) *Learned Optimism*. New York: Random House.

Selway, D. and Ashman, A. F. (1998) 'Disability, religion and health: a literature review in search of the spiritual dimensions of disability.' *Journal of Sociology and Social Welfare 26*, 125–142.

Sinclair, N. D. (1993) *Horrific Traumata: A Pastoral Response to the Post-traumatic Stress Disorder*. New York: Haworth Pastoral Press.

Sinha, D. (1965) 'Integration of modern psychology with Indian thought.' *Journal of Humanistic Psychology 6*, 21.

Slater, R. (1995) *The Psychology of Growing Old: Looking Forward*. Buckingham: Open University Press.

Smith, G. (1978) 'The meaning of success in social policy – a case study.' *Public Administration 56*, 263 ff.

Soderton, K. E. and Martinson, I. M. (1987) 'Patient spiritual coping strategies: a study of nurse and patient's perspective.' *Ecology Nursing Forum 14*, 41–46.

Souren, L. and Franssen, E. (1994) *Broken Connections: Alzheimer's Disease. Part 1 Origin and Course*. Lisse: Swets and Zeitlinger.

Spilka, B., Hood, R. W. Jr and Gorsuch, R. L. (1985) *The Psychology of Religion: An Empirical Perspective.* Englewood Cliffs, NJ: Prentice Hall.

Spilka, B., Shaver, P. and Kirkpatrick, L. A. (1985) 'A general attribution theory for the psychology of religion.' *Journal for the Scientific Study of Religion 24*, 1–20.

Sternberg, R. J. (ed) (1990) *Wisdom: Its Nature, Origins, and Development.* New York: Cambridge University Press.

Swinton, J. (2001) *Spiritual Maturity in the Later Years.* New York: Haworth Pastoral Press.

Szego, J. and Milburn, C. (2002) 'The death of ageing.' *The Age*, 6 April, 5.

Taylor, C. (2002) *Varieties of Religion Today: William James Revisited.* Cambridge, MA: Harvard University Press.

Teilhard de Chardin, P. (1999) *The Human Phenomenon.* Brighton: Academic Press.

Thomson, D. (2001) 'The getting and losing wisdom.' *Journal of Religious Gerontology 12*, 3/4, 111–112.

Thorson, J. A. and Cook, T. C. (eds) (1980) *Spiritual Well-being of the Elderly.* Springfield, IL: Charles C. Thomas.

Treetops, J. (1996) *Holy, Holy, Holy.* Leeds: Faith in Elderly People.

Turbott, J. (1996) 'Religion, spirituality and psychiatry: conceptual, cultural and personal challenges.' *Australian and New Zealand Journal of Psychiatry 30*, 720–727.

Underhill, E. (1993) *The Spiritual Life: Great Spiritual Truths for Everyday Life.* Oxford: Oneworld.

Ventis, W. L. (1995) 'The relationships between religion and mental health.' *Journal of Social Issues 51*, 2, 33–48.

Verma, S. (1998) 'The state of a healthy mind: the Indian world view.' *Journal of Indian Psychology 16*, 2, 1–9.

Vesti, P. and Kastrup, M. (1995) 'Treatment of torture survivors: psychosocial and somatic aspects.' In J. R. Freedy and S. E. Hobfall (eds) *Traumatic Stress: From Theory to Practice.* New York: Plenum Press.

Viney, L. (1993) *Life Stories: Personal Construct Therapy with the Elderly.* Chichester: Wiley.

Vrinte, R. (1996) *The Quest for the Inner Man: Transpersonal Psychotherapy and Integral Sadhana.* New Delhi: Motilal Banarasidas.

Walsh, K., King, M., Jones, L., Tookman, A. and Blizard, R. (2002) 'Bereavement and spiritual belief: prospective study.' *British Medical Journal 324*, 1551.

Walter, T. (1997) 'The ideology and organization of spiritual care: three approaches.' *Palliative Medicine 11*, 21–30.

Ward, R. A. (1984) *The Aging Experience: An Introduction to Social Gerontology*, 2nd edn. New York: Harper and Row.

Weaver, A. J., Koenig, H. G. and Ochberg, F. M. (1996) 'Posttraumatic stress, mental health professionals, and the clergy: a need for collaboration, training and research.' *Journal of Traumatic Stress 9*, 4, 847–856.

Weber, M. (1976) *The Protestant Ethic and the Rise of Capitalism*. London: George Allen and Unwin.

Webster, J. D. and Haight, B. K. (2002) *Critical Advances in Reminiscence Work: From Theory to Application*. New York: Springer.

Westgate, C. E. (1996) 'Spiritual wellness and depression.' *Journal of Counselling and Development 75*, 26–35.

Whitehead, E. E. and Whitehead, J. D. (1982) *Christian Life Patterns: The Psychological Challenges and Religious Invitations of Adult Life*. New York: Image Books, Doubleday.

Williams, D. R., Larson, D. B., Buckler, R. E. and Hackman, R. C. (1991) 'Religion and psychological distress in a community sample.' *Social Science and Medicine 32*, 1257–1262.

Williams, R. (2000a) *Lost Icons: Reflections on Cultural Bereavement*. Edinburgh: T. and T. Clark.

Williams, R. (2000b) *On Christian Theology*. Oxford: Blackwell.

Wilson, W. (1967) 'Correlates of avowed happiness.' *Psychological Bulletin 67*, 294–306.

Wolman, B. (1975) 'Principles of international psychotherapy.' *Psychotherapy: Theory, Research and Practice 12*, 149–159.

Woodward, K. (1991) *Ageing and its Discontents: Freud and Other Fictions*. Bloomington and Indianapolis: Indiana University Press.

Worthington, E. L. Jr, Kurusu, A. T., McCullough, M. E. and Sandage, J. S. (1996) 'Empirical research on religion and psychotherapeutic processes and outcomes: a 10-year review and research prospects.' *Psychological Bulletin 119*, 448–487.

Wright, S. G. and Sayre-Adams, J. (2000) *Sacred Space: Right Relationship and Spirituality in Health Care*. Edinburgh: Churchill Livingstone.

Wulff, D. M. (1996) 'The psychology of religion: an overview.' In E. P. Shafranske (ed) *Religion and the Clinical Practice of Psychology*. Washington, DC: American Psychological Association.

Yalom, I. D. (1980) *Existential Psychotherapy*. New York: Basic Books.

Young-Eisendrath, P. (ed) (2000) *The Psychology of Mature Spirituality*. London: Routledge.

Zabbia, K. (1996) *Painted Diaries*. Minneapolis: Fairview Press.

The Contributors

Kevin Barnard has been an Anglican priest for 24 years; he is Vicar of Bolsterstone in the diocese of Sheffield, where he acts as Bishop's Adviser on issues related to ageing.

Peter G. Coleman, after working as a researcher in the Netherlands, has spent the past 26 years at the University of Southampton where he is Professor of Psychogerontology. He has been involved in a multidisciplinary research project into ageing since 1977. He has written extensively on reminiscence and ageing.

Deborah Dunn is Priest-in-Charge of an Anglican church in Hilton, Western Australia, a chaplain in the Royal Australian Navy Reserve and part-time ecumenical chaplain at Alma Street Mental Health Centre in Fremantle. Her special interest is in spirituality and mental health issues in everyday living.

Malcolm Goldsmith recently retired as vicar of St Cuthbert's Episcopal Church, Colinton, Edinburgh, and was a former research fellow at the Stirling University Dementia Development Centre. He is author of *Hearing the Voice of People with Dementia* (Jessica Kingsley Publishers, 1996) and at the time of writing is working on a book on spirituality and dementia.

Rosalie Hudson, after postgraduate study in nursing and theology, spent 12 years as director of nursing in a 50-bed nursing home. She is associate professor in the School of Nursing, University of Melbourne, and has written extensively on dementia and death and dying.

David Jenkins was Professor of Theology and Religious Studies at the University of Leeds, 1979–84, and Bishop of Durham until his retirement in 1994. A Patron of the Christian Council on Ageing, he has recently published an account of his controversial life, entitled *The Calling of the Cuckoo*.

Albert Jewell was a Methodist minister for more than 40 years and Pastoral Director and Senior Chaplain with MHA Care Group from 1994 to 2001. During that time he co-ordinated the work of the Sir Halley Stewart Age Awareness Project and established MHA's centre for the spirituality of ageing in Leeds. He is the editor of *Sprirituality and Ageing* (Jessica Kingsley Publishers, 1999) and is currently researching how people cope with the transition from the 'third' to the 'fourth' ages of life.

John Killick, a former teacher, has been since 1992 writer-in-residence for Westminster Health Care and, since 1998, research fellow in communication through the arts in the Dementia Services Development Centre at the University of Stirling. His collections of poems have been published by *The Journal of Dementia Care* and he is co-author with Kate Allen of *Communication and the Care of People with Dementia.*

Ursula King was Professor of Theology and Religious Studies at the University of Bristol (1989–2002), where she is now Professor Emerita and senior research fellow. From 1998–2001 she was also visiting professor in Feminist Theology at the University of Oslo. Internationally known through her many publications and lectures, she is currently working on a new book on *Spirituality and Human Flourishing.*

Elizabeth MacKinlay, an Anglican priest, is senior lecturer at the University of Canberra and Director of the Centre for Ageing and Pastoral Studies there. She is the author of *The Spiritual Dimension of Ageing* (Jessica Kingsley Publishers, 2001).

Leo Missinne, a Catholic priest, belongs to the Society of Missionaries in Africa (White Fathers). Formerly dean and professor at the College of Psychology and Education at the University of Lovanium, Kinshasa, he is Professor of Gerontology at the University of Nebraska and visiting professor at various universities in North America, Asia and Europe.

Krishna Mohan is senior lecturer and co-ordinator of mental health research and services at Makerere University, Kampala, Uganda. His research at the time of writing includes the integration of eastern and western religious and spiritual approaches for health and psychotherapy.

Harriet Mowat was until recently Deputy Director of the Centre of Gerontology and Health Studies at Paisley University and editor of *Generations Review*. She previously worked in the Department of General Practice of Dundee University medical school. She has set up her own research consultancy, is honorary senior lecturer in practical theology at Aberdeen University and is much involved in the work of Spirited Scotland.

Penelope Wilcock is a former hospice chaplain and the author of *Spiritual Care of Dying and Bereaved People*. She has also written *The Hawk and the Dove*, a trilogy of books, the third of which explores in fiction the existential journey of a disabled man, further disabled by stroke, and of his friend. She works primarily with people outside the church or on its fringes, helping them to explore their own spirituality.

Subject
Index

Author Index

Macquarrie, J., 182
Maddi, S., 114
Maholick, L., 119
Mahoney, J.M., 173
Martinson, I.M., 179
Maton, K.I., 176
McCarthy, P., 165
McCulloch, A., 101, 106
McFadden, S., 173
McKinlay, A., 150-51
McNamara, L., 95
McSherry, W., 44
Merton, T., 128
Milburn, C., 90
Miller, J., 144, 147, 190
Mills, M., 101, 110
Missinne, L., 8, 15, 113-23, 218
Moberg, D.O., 44, 46, 49, 52, 53
Moffett, M., 35
Moffitt, L., 14, 24, 25, 149
Mohan, K., 8, 15, 161-79, 173, 218
Moody, H., 89
Mookherjee, H.N., 177
Moran, P., 176
Morton, I., 155
Mowat, H., 15, 42-57, 218
Musurillo, H., 195
Myers, D.G., 170, 176

Neame, A., 190
Neil, A., 178
Neuhaus, R., 90-91
Newman, J.H., 191
Nichol, D., 37
Norris, L., 79, 80
Nouwen, H.J.M., 87, 195
Nusberg, C., 162

Ochberg, F.M., 164
Orchard, H., 43, 44
Ornish, D., 174
Oropeza, M., 147

Palmer, K., 174
Paloutzian, R.F., 177
Pargament, K.I., 164, 175, 176, 179
Patricia, L.R., 176
Payne, I.R., 175, 177
Peck, S., 46
Pitskhelauri, G.Z., 161
Pope, A., 18
Post, S., 145, 151, 164
Potter, D., 72, 99
Pullman, P., 42

Quoist, M., 38

Rahner, K., 96
Reese, H.W., 165, 175
Reid, H., 44
Reker, G.T., 109
Reynolds, D.K., 109
Rilke, R.M., 123

Robinson, M., 27-28
Robshaw, V., 44
Robson, C., 57
Rosel, N., 107
Ross, J.L., 179
Rowe, J.W., 53
Ryan, D., 46
Ryan, S., 137

Sagy, S., 177
Sappington, A.A., 179
Sargent, N.M., 164
Sartre, J.-P., 113
Sayre-Adams, J., 87
Schafen, W.E., 176
Scheier, M.P., 175
Schick, F.L., 163
Schultz-Hipp, P.L., 18
Seeber, J., 52, 88
Seedhouse, D., 170
Seligman, M.E.P., 175
Selway, D., 176
Shaver, P., 175
Shield, B., 179
Sinclair, N,D., 164
Sinha, D., 172
Slater, R., 192, 195
Soderton, K.E., 179
Speck, P., 108
Speck, Rev Prebendary P., 101
Spilka, B., 164, 175
Sternberg, R.J., 79
Strauss, A.L., 74-75
Suh, D.K., 137
Swinton, J., 43, 51
Szego, J., 90

Taylor, C., 72, 111
Thérèse of Lisieux, St, 190
Thich Nhat Hanh, 66
Thomas, A., 108
Thomson, D., 79
Thomson, H., 51
Thorson, J.A., 8
Tolstoy, L., 114
Treetops, J., 92
Trevitt, C., 73, 76
Turbott, J., 178

Underhill, E., 131

Ventis, W.L., 177
Verma, S., 172
Vesti, P., 164
Viney, L., 34
Vrinte, R., 166, 167

Wallace, D., 8
Walsh, K., 44
Walter, T., 43, 44, 93
Ward, R.A., 163
Weaver, A.J., 164
Weber, M., 88-89
Webster, J.D., 106
Welsh, P., 166, 167

Westgate, C.E., 174
White, B., 47
Wilcock, P., 8, 15, 58-71, 218
Williams, D.R., 176
Williams, R.L., 93, 100, 163
Wilson, W., 169
Woman, B., 114
Wong, P.T.P., 109
Woodward, K., 56
Worthington, E.L., 165, 175
Wright, S.G., 87
Wulff, D.M., 164, 165, 178

Yalom, I.D., 113, 114, 119-20
Young-Eisendrath, P., 124

Zabbia, K., 151